GETTYSBURG:
The Final Fury

Also by Bruce Catton

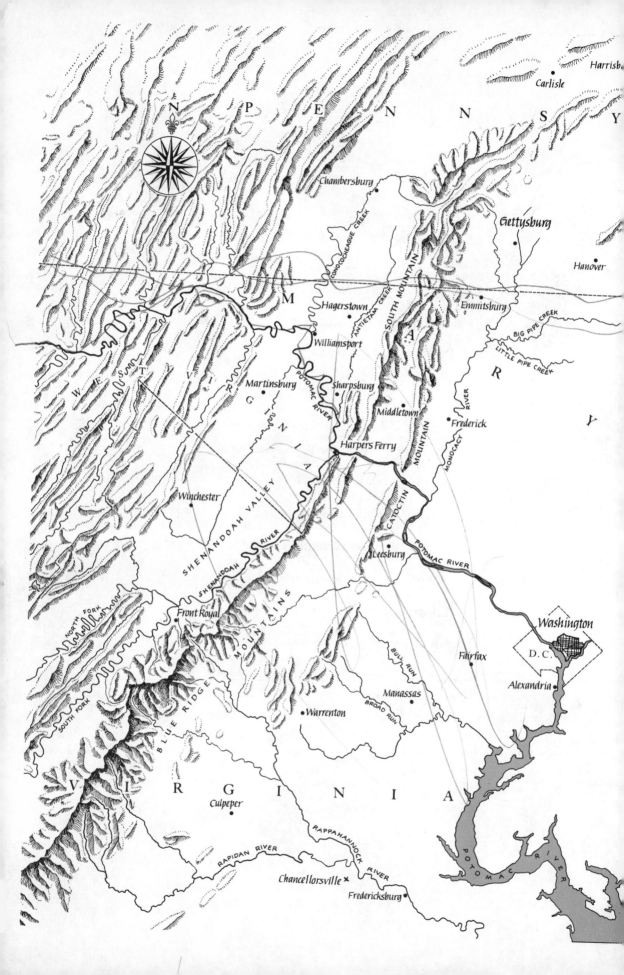

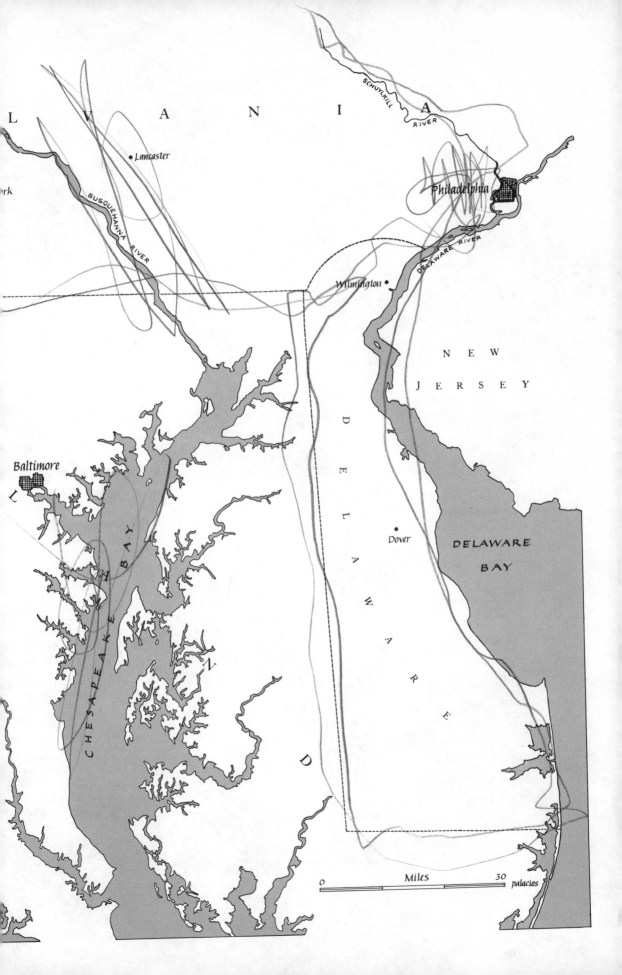

SCHUYLKILL RIVER

• Lancaster

Philadelphia

York

SUSQUEHANNA RIVER

DELAWARE RIVER

Wilmington •

N E W

J E R S E Y

Baltimore

L

C H E S A P E A K E   B A Y

Dover •

DELAWARE
BAY

D
E
L
A
W
A
R
E

N

D

Miles

0   30   palacios

BRUCE CATTON

GETTYSBURG:
The Final Fury

DOUBLEDAY
NEW YORK LONDON TORONTO SYDNEY AUCKLAND

A Main Street Book
PUBLISHED BY DOUBLEDAY
a division of Bantam Doubleday Dell Publishing Group, Inc.
1540 Broadway, New York, New York 10036

Main Street Books, Doubleday, and the portrayal of a
building with a tree are trademarks of Doubleday, a division of
Bantam Doubleday Dell Publishing Group, Inc.

All photographs, drawings, and paintings reproduced
in this book are from the collections of the Library of
Congress, except the two on pages 9 and 100, which are
reproduced by courtesy of The Bettmann Archive, Inc.
The maps are by Rafael Palacios.

Library of Congress Cataloging-in-Publication Data
Catton, Bruce, 1899–
    Gettysburg: the final fury / Bruce Catton.
        p. cm.
    Originally published: 1974.
    1. Gettysburg, Battle of, 1863.
    I. Title.
E475.53.C32   1990   89-23554
973.7'349—dc20   CIP
ISBN 0-385-41145-6

Copyright © 1974 by Bruce Catton
ALL RIGHTS RESERVED
PRINTED IN THE UNITED STATES OF AMERICA
APRIL 1990

10 9 8 7 6 5 4

CONTENTS

ILLUSTRATIONS

MAPS

GETTYSBURG:
The Final Fury

I

The Road to Gettysburg

It took a strange combination of forces to bring about the terrible battle of Gettysburg. No one of these, taken by itself, was strong enough to cause such a cataclysm. Only when they were arranged together in proper sequence did these forces become deadly. The elements that make up gunpowder are harmless enough, separately; in combination they become explosive, needing only a spark or a sudden jar to set them off. The battle of Gettysburg was like that.

It was compounded partly of geography, which is to say that the armies fought at Gettysburg because the roads led them there. Sheer chance played its part in this; if various circumstances had been just a little different the unremarkable Pennsylvania market town would have remained at peace and the armies would have gone elsewhere. Military logic was responsible, in part, and so was plain human miscalculation, because it is not always easy to interpret the date that logic brings you.

Finally, the battle was fated, in that it grew out of what the war for two years had been. It was a battle that had to be fought, and the forces that produced it were so stupendous that the battle became the great hinge of the war, the turning point where it began to swing in a different direction. But even though destiny was at work, it is still worth while to see why this great fight took place at Gettysburg instead of in some other town, on the first three days of July 1863 instead of at some other time.

Gettysburg came just two months after the most dazzling of all

Confederate victories, the battle of Chancellorsville, where the Army of Northern Virginia under Robert E. Lee, who was brilliantly aided by Stonewall Jackson, defeated the Federal Army of the Potomac under Major General Joe Hooker. The Federals outnumbered the Confederates here, two to one, but Lee and Jackson between them were more than a dozen Joe Hookers could have handled, and the Federal offensive which had been supposed to capture Richmond ended in an ignominious retreat. Yet if this Confederate triumph was a work of high military art, it was actually worth less than it seemed to be worth. For one thing, Jackson was killed, and Lee's army was never again the instantly responsive precision instrument it had been. In the second place, Lee was still badly outnumbered, and the Federal army had great recuperative power; left to itself it would inevitably renew the offensive and the whole job would have to be done over again. Chancellorsville had settled nothing; it had simply set the stage for a further struggle.

In addition, if things had been going well for the Confederacy in Virginia, they had been going very badly in the Mississippi Valley. While Lee was defeating Hooker, Major General U. S. Grant was forcing his way into the open country behind the great Confederate fortress of Vicksburg, and by the end of the third week in May he had the Confederate Lieutenant General John Pemberton and his army firmly locked up in Vicksburg, isolated and under siege. Unless somebody came to Pemberton's rescue and forced Grant to raise the siege, Vicksburg was bound to fall, and when it fell the Federals would control the entire Mississippi River. If that happened the Confederacy would be well on its way toward final defeat.

So when the Confederate authorities took stock, late in May of 1863, they could see dire emergency taking shape in the West, and that fact was bound to affect any plans that might be made for the use of Lee's army. The Secretary of War proposed that Lee detach a division of infantry and send it off to Pemberton's rescue. The division suggested for this move was one commanded by young Major General George Pickett, attached to the I Corps commanded by Lieutenant General James Longstreet. Longstreet was a solid, dependable fighting

4

man, Lee's most trusted lieutenant now that Jackson was gone, and Longstreet considered Pickett's his best division. Lee strongly objected to this proposal, and he warned the Secretary of War that if this was the only way to save Vicksburg, the government would have to make up its mind whether it wanted to lose Mississippi or Virginia; and the fact that the Confederacy could not under any circumstances afford to lose either state simply added to the load carried by President Jefferson Davis, who would have to make the decision. Lee believed that Hooker was being reinforced and would soon resume the offensive; his own responsibility was the defense of Virginia and the Confederate capital, and he naturally did not think he ought to be weakened.

As a matter of fact, some of President Davis's advisers thought that Vicksburg ought to be saved even if that meant taking long chances in front of Richmond. The distinguished General P. G. T. Beauregard, now commanding in South Carolina, urged that Lee be sent to Tennessee, taking Longstreet's corps with him, to take command of the Confederate army near Chattanooga commanded by General Braxton Bragg. Using Bragg's army thus augmented, Beauregard believed, Lee could stage an offensive in Tennessee that would compel the Federal government to recall Grant from Mississippi. As for Virginia—the Army of the Potomac was notoriously slow to act, and the depleted Army of Northern Virginia could probably hold it off until Lee and Longstreet's corps returned. Longstreet advanced a similar plan, except that his plan did not involve sending Lee himself to Tennessee.

In the end none of these proposals was adopted. The Confederates in the West would have to get along as best they could, and Lee—well, Lee had a daring plan of his own. He would invade Pennsylvania.

It was a bold move, bound to bring the war to a climax, and yet the reasons for it are somewhat obscure.

Then and afterward it was argued that Lee's invasion would relieve the desperate situation in Mississippi by forcing President Lincoln to withdraw support from General Grant. This argument simply does not stand up. The siege of Vicksburg began on May 19. Lee could not put his army in motion before June, and it would be the end of June before he could hope to cross the Potomac. This was giving General Grant altogether too much time; and if Lincoln wanted reinforcements to meet Lee's thrust, he would not have to reach all the way to Mississippi to get them.

It was also held that the invasion would support a Southern peace offensive. There was much war-weariness in the North, and the presence of a Confederate army in Pennsylvania would add to it—perhaps to the point where Lincoln would be forced to concede Southern independence. (The invasion might also enable the Confederacy to grasp that elusive will-o'-the-wisp British recognition.) But this would work only if Lee won an overwhelming victory in Pennsylvania. Anything short of that would only stimulate Northern energies. After all, Lee had invaded the northland in September of 1862 and had won neither a negotiated peace nor recognition by London. Instead he had been thrown back at Antietam (Sharpsburg) and Lincoln issued the Emancipation Proclamation as a direct result.

Actually, Lee's reasons for marching north seem to have been fairly simple. Sooner or later the Army of the Potomac would resume its drive on Richmond; to move north would disrupt the enemy's war plans and throw Hooker off balance; it might very well delay the renewed Yankee invasion until the following year. The Confederacy was hard pressed, and that would be a gain worth making.

In addition, the move would at least give Virginia temporary relief from a strain that had become almost intolerable. The constant struggling of the rival armies had laid much of the state waste; if the war could be moved north for a time that would be a distinct advantage, and Lee's army could draw its supplies of meat and grain from the lush farmlands of Pennsylvania. Let the North support the war for a while; Virginia needed a chance to catch its breath.

In plain English, then, the invasion was a matter of limited objectives, which might be summed up in the remark that since Lee's army was going to have to fight somewhere this summer, it might better fight north of the Mason and Dixon line than south of it.

The only trouble with this was that because Lee and his army were what they were, an invasion with limited objectives was not possible. If this army went north of the Potomac, its venture was going to be an all-or-nothing thrust simply because both friend and foe were bound to look at it that way. Lee and the Army of Northern Virginia had won too many battles; they had begun to seem invincible, both to their enemies and also to themselves. When they went north they carried the undeveloped climax of the war with them. Win or lose, this march was going to take them to the high-water mark.

The one strategist who realized this most clearly was that untaught, awkward, non-military man Abraham Lincoln.

Lincoln had had no military education before he entered the White House, but he was a man who could learn fast, and by the summer of 1863 he could understand a military equation as well as any man in America. In the late spring of 1863, when something like panic went across the North at the news that Lee was invading Pennsylvania, Lincoln saw in the move a bright opportunity for the Federals. Coming north, Lee was exposing his army to destruction. The Federals always had the advantage in numbers; now they would have the advantage in position as well, and if they maneuvered skillfully they could cut this invading army off, hem it in, and destroy it utterly. . . . That, at any rate, is the way Lincoln saw it, and his hopes rose. Grant obviously was going to take Vicksburg. If at the same time the great Army of Northern Virginia could be taken off the board, the war would be about over.

Lee's army at the end of May lay south of the Rappahannock River, in and near Fredericksburg, with Hooker's army just north of the river keeping watch. Contrary to Lee's expectation, Hooker was not being reinforced; actually, he was losing strength because the time of a number of his volunteer regiments was expiring and thousands of good soldiers were being paid off and sent home. He still had an advantage in numbers, but his army and Lee's were more nearly on a parity in strength than they had ever been before or would be again. Lee had probably 75,000 men of all arms; Hooker may have had between 85,-000 and 90,000, and Hooker's men were much better equipped and fed. As a counterweight to this, Lee's men had the habit of victory, and Hooker's had never been able to acquire that habit. All in all, the armies were fairly close to equal.

Lee's march began on June 3, when Longstreet's I Corps faded back from the Rappahannock crossings and marched northwest toward Culpeper Courthouse, to be followed a day or so later by the II Corps led by Lieutenant General Richard Ewell. Ewell was a bald, peppery little man with a wooden leg—he had been maimed during the preliminaries to the second battle of Bull Run—and when the army was on the march he rode in a buggy. In battle he mounted his horse, game leg and all, and had himself strapped to the saddle.

For rear guard at Fredericksburg, Lee left his III Infantry Corps under Lieutenant General A. P. Hill, one of the Confederacy's fabulous fighting men. It was not long before Hooker saw what was happening and proposed to attack Hill in force, driving him off and moving directly on Richmond. President Lincoln overruled him, pointing out that Lee's army rather than the Confederate capital was Hooker's proper objective now. Hooker began to move northwest on a course roughly parallel with Lee's, keeping the Army of the Potomac always between Lee and Washington.

Lee's plan was simple. He would move beyond the Blue Ridge, cross the Potomac, and then march toward the east, threatening Philadelphia and Baltimore, cutting Washington's communications with the rest of the country, and putting on pressure that would force Hooker to attack him; in effect, he would blend offensive strategy with defensive tactics, compelling his opponent (as he had so often done before) to fight his kind of fight. At Chancellorsville Hooker had shown himself to be erratic when the heat was on. When the armies met in Pennsylvania the heat would be greater than anything Hooker had experienced before. Limited objectives or no, the possibilities for Lee were dazzling.

On the surface, everything went smoothly. Lee handled the northward march most competently, and Hooker never had a good chance to attack him en route. Longstreet held his corps in and east of the Blue Ridge, Ewell smashed a Federal outpost at Winchester and then moved boldly north, across Maryland and into Pennsylvania; Hill fol-

This wartime lithograph, "Lee and His Generals," does show a great many Confederate generals, although many of them were not especially associated with Lee (except that they all fought on the same side). Lee of course is in the center. The more prominent other generals include P. G. T. Beauregard, mounted, at left, with Braxton Bragg over his right shoulder; Joseph E. Johnston, raising his hat, with heavily bearded Jeb Stuart on his right. Mounted, on Lee's left, is James Longstreet, followed (to the right, in background) by Bedford Forrest, John B. Hood, and A. P. Hill. Mounted in the right foreground, is Stonewall Jackson; mounted, by Jackson's right elbow, is Richard Ewell. (The Bettmann Archive, Inc.)

By the night of June 28 Lee learned two things—that the Army of the Potomac was north of the Potomac River, instead of lying inert to the south of it as he had supposed, and that Meade had replaced Hooker as its commander. He at once ordered his army to assemble at the handiest place, which turned out to be Gettysburg. Meade, meanwhile, ordered his own army to concentrate along a little stream called Pipe Creek, which offered a good defense position covering both Washington and Baltimore, while his cavalry under Buford rode north to get a line on Lee's position. Stuart's Confederate cavalry, meanwhile, was trying desperately to regain its proper position on Lee's immediate right flank.

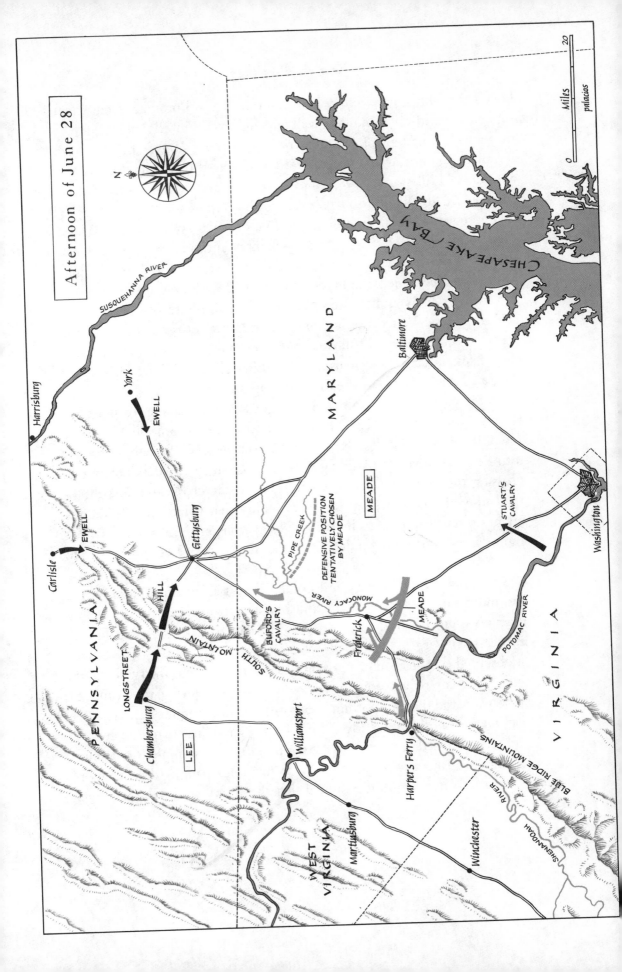

Afternoon of June 28

N

PENNSYLVANIA

Harrisburg

SUSQUEHANNA RIVER

Carlisle
EWELL

York
EWELL

Gettysburg

HILL

Chambersburg

LONGSTREET

LEE

SOUTH MOUNTAIN

BUFORD'S CAVALRY

PIPE CREEK

Williamsport

Martinsburg

WEST VIRGINIA

Winchester

SHENANDOAH RIVER

BLUE RIDGE MOUNTAINS

Harpers Ferry

POTOMAC RIVER

VIRGINIA

MONOCACY RIVER

Frederick
MEADE

DEFENSIVE POSITION
TENTATIVELY CHOSEN
BY MEADE

MEADE

MARYLAND

Baltimore

CHESAPEAKE BAY

STUART'S CAVALRY

Washington

Miles
palacios
0   20

lowed with his corps, and when he crossed the Potomac, Longstreet slipped beyond the mountain wall and followed him. By the final days of June, Lee had all of his infantry and artillery above the Potomac. Ewell had gone far to the eastward and was threatening Harrisburg and York. Hill was ready to move after him, and Longstreet had his men posted at Chambersburg, awaiting developments.

There was a slight question about Lee's cavalry. It was led by Major General J. E. B. ("Jeb") Stuart—flamboyant, picturesque, a head-line-hunter, but an uncommonly able cavalry leader for all that: a man on whom Lee relied implicitly. Stuart had a double assignment—to screen Lee's army and to keep Lee informed all the time where Hooker's army was. When the last of Lee's infantry crossed the Potomac, Stuart was supposed to follow it and then move eastward along Lee's right flank, covering the march and making certain that Lee knew just where all the elements of the Federal army might be.

Preparing to leave Virginia, Stuart got Lee's permission to put a little extra frill on his march. The Federal army lay in camp in Virginia a few miles east of the Blue Ridge, and Stuart believed he could best get into Pennsylvania by marching entirely around this Federal army and crossing the Potomac far downstream from the crossings Lee's infantry had used. Lee approved, stipulating only that whatever he did, Stuart must get promptly to his assigned position on the invading army's right flank. On this march deep into enemy territory Lee simply had to have Stuart near him.

Stuart moved on June 25 and immediately ran into trouble. Hooker had moved up to the Potomac, and his huge army occupied all of the river crossings Stuart had planned to use. Stuart was crowded far off into eastern Virginia, Hooker got his entire army north of the river unobserved, and instead of rejoining Lee's army within thirty-six hours Stuart did not regain contact for a solid week. During that time—in some ways the most important week in his whole military career—Lee was in effect a blind man. He did not know where his enemies were.

To make matters worse, Stuart's reputation for complete reliability led Lee to make a false assumption. When days passed with no word from Stuart, Lee naturally assumed that the Army of the Potomac was inactive, remaining in its camps in Virginia; if it were on the move, Stuart would surely send word, as he had always done in the past. (Lee of course had no idea that Stuart had been blocked out of the play altogether.) If Hooker remained inactive south of the Potomac, the invading Confederates, far north of the river, could do things they would not have ventured to do if their foes were in close pursuit. So by June 28 Lee had his army spread out over a forty-five-mile crescent, Lee himself with Longstreet's corps at Chambersburg, Ewell in York and on the river bank opposite Harrisburg, Hill moving east eight or ten miles from Chambersburg. The army was dangerously dispersed, but with the Army of the Potomac south of the river this was safe enough.

Then, that evening, Lee learned that Hooker's entire army was massed in the vicinity of Frederick, Maryland. It was closer to the separate pieces of Lee's army than those pieces were to each other. Lee would be destroyed if he did not concentrate at once.

So Confederate couriers galloped off along the Pennsylvania roads that night, calling the scattered legions together. The army would assemble at Gettysburg—at Gettysburg, and not elsewhere, simply because it was central and the roads led there. The first of the accidents that would make Gettysburg a battleground had taken place. Lee's soldiers hurried as if drawn there by a magnet.

And so, for that matter, did the leading divisions of the Army of the Potomac. They were no more interested in Gettysburg than Lee's men were. They were just groping for the enemy and this town seemed the handiest place to go groping. And as June came to an end, fate was driving thousands of soldiers toward the point of deadly collision.

II

First Day: Collision

The Federal soldiers who moved toward Gettysburg were Hooker's army no longer. As they trudged along through the choking dust and the thick summer heat they were under the command of Major General George Gordon Meade, chosen by the government at Washington to replace Hooker at the moment when the greatest battle of the war was obviously just about to take place.

Hooker had been a dashing, competent soldier as leader of a division and, later, of an army corps, but the top command had somehow been too much for him. Under pressure he had simply folded up; he had fumbled his way to defeat at Chancellorsville because the responsibility of high command had paralyzed his professional faculties, and the failure had been so clearly a failure of his own nerve that he had lost the confidence of President Lincoln, not to mention that of Secretary of War Edwin M. Stanton and General in Chief Henry W. Halleck.

They had made up their minds to relieve him, but finding a qualified successor was difficult and it was not until the Confederate campaign of invasion was clearly approaching its climax that the change was finally made. They selected General Meade, who had been in command of the V Army Corps, largely because he was known as a reliable professional soldier who did not scare easily.

Outside of the V Corps, the soldiers had hardly so much as heard of him, and he definitely was not the inspirational leader who arouses the enthusiasm of the rank and file. To use a modern expression, he utterly lacked charisma. He was crusty, not to say crabbed, with a quick temper and a sharp tongue, and he once remarked without rancor that he had heard soldiers refer to him as a "damned goggle-eyed snapping turtle." But if his inspirational qualities were nil and his strategic abilities were unknown, there definitely was nothing wrong with his nerves. He was not afraid of the weight of top command and he was not in the least afraid of Robert E. Lee, and it soon developed that when they chose Meade the authorities acted very wisely indeed.

Meade had to defend Washington, along with Philadelphia, Baltimore, and the rest of the northland, and the only way to do this was to bring Lee to battle and defeat him. Somewhat strung out, Lee's army was moving eastward, and Meade did not know exactly where it was or what Lee had in mind. Sensibly enough, Meade concluded that if he found a substantial piece of this army and prodded it vigorously, the separate parts would come together quickly enough. Then Lee would have to give battle because of the conditions under which he was operating.

Lee maintained contact with his base in Virginia, but to all intents and purposes he had abandoned his supply line and was living on the country. This Pennsylvania farm country was rich and Lee's army had had no trouble collecting food and forage—it was in fact living rather high just now—but there was one catch to all this. To live thus, the invading army had to keep moving, because if it stayed in one place very long it would consume all the supplies its immediate neighborhood produced. So far the army had kept on the march and had had no problems, but if Meade could compel it to concentrate it could not wait for him to make the attack. It would have to take the offensive or retreat; with luck, Meade would be able to make Lee attack him on ground of Meade's own choosing.

To find a suitable fragment of Lee's army, Meade sent Major General John Buford's division of cavalry north to cut across what appeared to be Lee's line of march. To molest the troops that Buford was likely to find, Meade chose Major General John Reynolds and gave him command of about one third of the army—Reynolds' own I Corps, Major General Oliver Otis Howard's XI Corps, and the III Corps under Major General Dan Sickles. On the last day of June

18

When Gettysburg is studied as a problem in strategy and tactics, attention is usually focused on General Robert E. Lee. This does some injustice to the Union commander, Major General George Gordon Meade; for if Lee lost the battle, Meade was the man who won it, and the Union cause owed a great deal to the cool competence with which he handled his army. For the first time the Army of the Potomac was under a man who refused to get nervous or uncertain when he confronted Lee on the battlefield. Meade was not a man who scared easily. . . . He is shown here in a picture made some time before Gettysburg; he wears a major general's shoulder straps but they have been tacked on to a brigadier general's coat.

Buford got into Gettysburg and discovered that a large body of Confederate infantry lay a few miles to the west, astride the Chambersburg road. Buford strung dismounted troopers out in a battle line on one of the low ridges a mile or so west of Gettysburg, ordered patrols off to the north to check on reports that additional Confederates were coming down from Carlisle, and sent word of all this to Reynolds, who was a short distance south of Gettysburg. Reynolds ordered his men to march for Gettysburg, and on the morning of July 1 he spurred on ahead of them to meet Buford, to get all the news Buford had, and to see for himself how the situation was developing.

It was developing fast, and fighting had already begun. Buford's troopers were firing at an advancing line of Confederate infantry, artillery had gone into action on both sides, and while Buford's men were holding the Confederates in check they obviously could not do so much longer; in a situation like this, cavalry could not hope to do much more than delay advancing infantry and force it to send out a formal line of battle. Reynolds conferred with Buford on the grounds of a Lutheran seminary near the Chambersburg road, concluded that this was a good place for a fight, and sent couriers off to bring in the leading elements of the on-coming I Corps.

The first Federal troops to come up were good ones—Brigadier General James Wadsworth's division, which included the famous Iron Brigade: western troops, known as one of the stoutest fighting units in the army. Reynolds put the westerners south of the Chambersburg road, sent Wadsworth's other brigade into action north of the road, had Buford withdraw his cavalry, and made it clear that if the Confederates wanted to occupy that ridge they would have to fight for it.

It speedily became clear that this was just what the Southerners proposed to do. They belonged to A. P. Hill's III Corps, and Hill was one of the most pugnacious soldiers in either army—tense, impetuous, a man who liked to force the fighting regardless of consequences, coming in now in the style of a heads-down slugger always willing to take a blow in order to land one. Hill had no especial reason to get into Gettysburg, but he did not need one; there were armed Yankees in front of him offering to fight, and he was going to accept their offer without

Because rifled muskets gave infantry greatly increased fire power, the day of massed cavalry attacks on foot soldiers in the style of the Napoleonic wars had passed by the 1860s. Dismounted cavalrymen, however, could stand off an infantry attack long enough to compel the infantry commander to deploy his men in battle order, thereby displaying his strength and his intentions, and so it was on the morning of the first day's fighting at Gettysburg. On the ridges west of town, Union cavalry commander Brigadier General John Buford put his cavalry in action against Confederate infantry of Lieutenant General A. P. Hill's III Corps, delaying the Confederate advance just long enough to permit Union infantry to reach the scene. When cavalrymen fought on foot, one man in every four was detailed to hold the horses a short distance behind the fighting line; the other three used their carbines dismounted, acting precisely like infantry.

On July 1 Hill's III Corps struck Meade's advanced infantry, the I Corps under Reynolds, just west of Gettysburg. Howard's XI Corps came up to help the Federals just as Ewell's II Corps struck the Union flank from north and northeast. By mid-afternoon the Federals had been driven through Gettysburg and were holding on to high ground just south of the town. Lee was bringing up the rest of his army, while Meade was hurrying his own infantry to the scene.

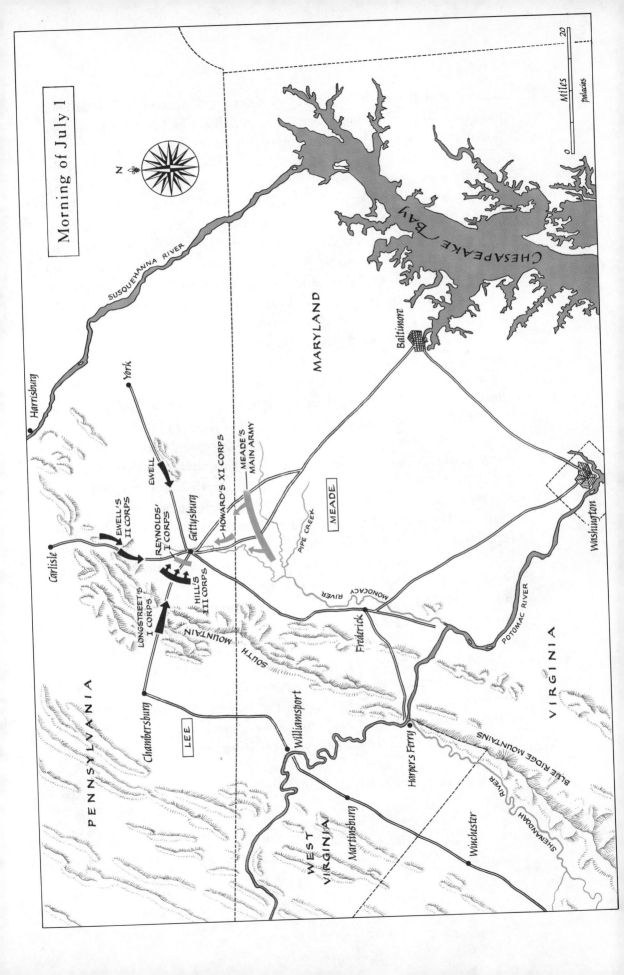

Morning of July 1

N

CHESAPEAKE BAY

SUSQUEHANNA RIVER

MARYLAND

Harrisburg

York

Baltimore

EWELL

EWELL'S
II CORPS

Carlisle

REYNOLDS'
I CORPS

Gettysburg

HOWARD'S XI CORPS

MEADE'S
MAIN ARMY

MEADE

LONGSTREET'S
I CORPS

HILL'S
III CORPS

PIPE CREEK

SOUTH MOUNTAIN

Chambersburg

LEE

Frederick

MONOCACY RIVER

Washington

POTOMAC RIVER

VIRGINIA

Williamsport

Harpers Ferry

BLUE RIDGE MOUNTAINS

WEST
VIRGINIA

Martinsburg

SHENANDOAH RIVER

Winchester

PENNSYLVANIA

Miles
palacios

0   20

delay and that was that. In place of the routine sparring that had been going on when Reynolds rode up to get Buford's situation report, an uncommonly savage battle was rapidly developing.

Reynolds did not live to see much of it. He rode forward to get the Iron Brigade lined up against Hill's advancing infantry, in the woods and fields of a farm owned by a man named McPherson, and some Confederate sharpshooter in Mr. McPherson's barn drew a bead on him and shot him dead. Reynolds might have had command of the Army of the Potomac—it appears that the job was definitely offered to him not long after the battle of Chancellorsville—but he did not want it because he believed the War Department interfered with the army's commander too much; he said so and the job went to Meade, and now Reynolds was killed in the opening moments of the battle he had helped to bring on.

Command of the I Army Corps passed temporarily to the senior division commander, Major General Abner Doubleday, and as fast as fresh Union troops came up Doubleday fed them into action. A Confederate attack south of the Chambersburg road was beaten back sharply, and a Confederate brigade trying to advance through a railroad cut north of the road was broken up with heavy loss; but Hill had more men than Doubleday had and he kept piling them in relentlessly, and while the Federals held their ground tenaciously, they suffered fearful casualties. Before the day ended the Iron Brigade had been wrecked, one of its regiments having lost 80 per cent of its numbers, and the whole I Corps had been so badly mangled that it was never again really effective as a combat force. During the following winter it was broken up, with its survivors distributed among other corps.

Until noon and past, the Union I Corps managed to hold its ground. Then a new pressure developed—a powerful battle line of Confederate infantry, marching south from the general direction of Carlisle: Major General Robert Rodes's division of Ewell's II Corps, coming in on the Federal right flank as neatly as if it had all been planned in advance.

Federal reinforcements came up just in time, Howard's XI Corps hurrying up from the south on the double in response to the messages Reynolds sent out before he died. Howard conferred briefly with Doubleday, took general command, by seniority, of all the troops present, planted one of his brigades as reserve on Cemetery Hill, the high ground just south of Gettysburg, and sent the rest of his corps into the open country north of town to meet Rodes's attack. For a time the situation was stabilized, and an enlarged battle rolled and crashed across the Pennsylvania countryside, the two Federal corps making a line that ran north and south along the ground of the morning's fight and then bent eastward at right angles in an improvised line that could hold temporarily but was by no means strong enough to meet any additional pressure.

Additional pressure came at once. Among the odd chances that combined to bring about a major battle at Gettysburg was the fact that Lee's order for a concentration of the army brought his troops into the Gettysburg area at the precise times and places where they could do the Federals the most harm. Now it was another of Ewell's divisions, commanded by the dour fighting man Major General Jubal Early, hurrying westward from York, that found itself coming into battle when and where it was most needed. It struck Howard's exposed right flank and lapped over into the area behind him, and Early ordered a vigorous advance. Howard's men had had all they could do to stave off the attack from the north. Before this new assault they were helpless.

By the oddest chance Lee himself reached the scene shortly before this happened. He had started eastward from Chambersburg in the morning, with Longstreet's corps preparing to take the road behind him; hearing the sound of Hill's battle, Lee had spurred on ahead, and he rode up to Hill's field headquarters and got a size-up of the situation. He concluded at once that this fight ought not to be pressed any farther just now. He had no idea where the rest of Meade's army was, less than half of his own army was on the scene, and it seemed to him that it would be rash to bring on a finish fight until he had all of his own forces in hand and knew where the bulk of the opposing force might be. He told Hill not to press the offensive—and just then the arrival of Early's division caught the Federals in the flank. Ewell's third

Death of Reynolds
Gettysburg

The first Federal infantry to reach the battlefield was Major General John F. Reynolds' I Army Corps. Meade had ordered Reynolds forward to determine whether Gettysburg was a suitable place for a battle and gave him temporary control of the III and XI Corps besides his own. Reynolds had his men relieve Buford's overmatched cavalry and opened a hot fight along Seminary Ridge and astride a railway cutting north of the Chambersburg road; he ordered the other infantry forward and sent word to Meade that Gettysburg was a good place to fight. Having done this, he rode forward to arrange his battle line and was shot dead by a Confederate sharpshooter. An enlisted man who rode with him as his orderly said later that he had seen many men killed in the war but that he never saw a man die as quickly as did Reynolds. Apparently the general was lifeless before his body struck the ground.

For the most part, the story of the July 1 fighting at Gettysburg is a story of unrelieved defeat for the Federal troops, but during the morning hours there were moments of triumph. One of these came when Southern troops tried to advance down an unfinished railroad cutting north of the Chambersburg road and were overpowered and compelled to surrender. The artist who made this sketch wrote that he followed the description of a Union Officer who was engaged here and who said that Brigadier General James J. Archer's Confederate brigade was the one that ran into trouble; the artist himself was doubtful that the capture took place here. Apparently Archer himself was taken prisoner south of the Chambersburg road, but his brigade—which was in Major General Harry Heth's division of the III Corps—did lose some 500 men captured in the first day's fight and the railroad cutting was the only place where any appreciable number of Confederates were taken prisoner on that day.

27

division was not far away, Longstreet's troops were on the road and would be up in a few hours; here was what looked very much like a decisive victory taking shape under the smoke clouds to the north and east—and Lee instantly reversed himself and ordered a general offensive by everybody in sight.

So the battle flared up anew and the Federals were overwhelmed. Howard's corps was simply swamped, and though valiant rear-guard elements bought as much time as they could, the corps as a whole had to retreat pell-mell through Gettysburg to temporary safety on Cemetery Hill. When these men retreated, Doubleday's men could not hold their ground because the exultant Confederates were storming in behind them and attacking them furiously from in front as well. After a bitter last-ditch struggle around the Lutheran seminary, these Federals took off for Gettysburg, ran through the disorderly town (full of battle smoke and lost soldiers, bullets flying in every direction, victors and defeated mingling in a confused, bewildering turmoil), and made their way to Cemetery Hill and the long ridge that ran south from it, aligning their right flank with Howard's left.

While all this was happening, Reynolds' messages had reached Meade, who had his headquarters fifteen miles to the south, and Meade at once acted to pull his army together. Learning that Reynolds had been killed, Meade sent Major General Winfield S. Hancock, commander of the II Corps, hurrying into Gettysburg with orders to assume general command there and to determine whether Gettysburg was a suitable place for the all-out fight with Lee that Meade was determined to fight sooner or later.

Hancock came up just as the beaten Federals were assembling on the high ground south of Gettysburg. He seems to have had a brief dispute with Howard, who ranked him and who did not see why he himself should not continue to command this part of Meade's army, but Hancock was a burly, energetic man who took this in his stride. He established his own authority, got the broken fragments of the I and XI Corps into position as best he could, sent word to Meade that Gettysburg would be a very good place to have a battle, and settled down to hold on until the rest of the army came up.

Hancock "The Superb"

When he learned that Reynolds had been killed, General Meade sent Major General Winfield S. Hancock forward to take charge at Gettysburg. Hancock reached the scene early in the afternoon of July 1, just in time to see the over-matched Unionists driven away from their positions north and west of town. He determined that the high ground below Gettysburg—Culp's Hill, Cemetery Hill, and the long stretch of Cemetery Ridge running south to the Round Tops—could and should be held. He organized what troops were at hand to hold this ground and sent word of his decision to Meade, who promptly ordered the rest of the army to Gettysburg and came on himself, reaching the scene around midnight. Here is a studio picture of Hancock; "Hancock the Superb," newspaper writers called him, one of the dominant actors in the Union army's greatest victory.

If what Hancock feared was a renewal late that afternoon of the Confederate assault, he was agreeably disappointed, because the assault was not renewed. Confederate survivors argued about this for years to come—indeed, the argument is still going on, in the books—and Lee's admirers have always asserted that a great chance was missed because General Ewell failed to follow up the day's triumph with a sweeping assault on the disorganized Federals who were taking refuge on Cemetery Hill. Certainly the Federals had been roughly handled—between them, the two corps had lost close to half of their strength and it took time to get the fugitives sorted out and put into position for a new fight—and if Ewell's men could have followed up their victory by surging on through the town and storming the insecure defenses on the heights, a momentous battle might have been won. In the years since July 1, 1863, a great deal of criticism has descended on General Dick Ewell.

Most of the criticism is undeserved. It is true enough that for half an hour or so after the first Federals reached the high ground, the Federal army was not in good shape to stand off a vigorous attack, but it is mortally hard to see how such an attack could have been made. Ewell's men just were not in shape to make it on the heels of the Federal retreat. Rodes's division had suffered extremely heavy losses, Early's was temporarily disorganized by the pursuit through town, Ewell's third division was just beginning to come up, and during the half hour or so when the opportunity was really at its best, an attack was not quite practicable. Later in the day it might indeed have been made, but by that time the Federals probably were able to hold their ground. They held a strong defensive position, reinforcements were on their way, and it is probably true that by the time the Confederates were ready to launch an assault the opportunity had passed.

As a matter of fact, Lee was on the scene, and if he had felt that an assault was in order he could have ordered it. He did not do so; nor did he join in the criticism of Ewell after the battle. He did indicate that he believed something, somehow, had been missed when he said, long afterward, that if he had had Stonewall Jackson with him, he would have won the battle of Gettysburg; but to say that Ewell was not

Stonewall's equal was not necessarily to criticize him. Nobody else was, either.

In any case, when night came the armies stayed where they were, Federals on the hills south of Gettysburg, Confederates arrayed on the rolling country to the north and west. For whatever it was worth, the town itself was in Confederate possession, but this fight was not waged for possession of a town. It had begun as an almost accidental collision between two armies, it had continued because sheer force of circumstances made it impossible to break it off, and it was actually fought for possession of control over the future of America.

III

Second Day:
Fighting by Compulsion

On the morning of July 2 General Robert E. Lee appeared to be on the crest of the wave. He had won a smashing victory, he had his army in hand now, and there was good reason to suppose that he would complete the triumph today. By nightfall Confederate independence might well be very near.

Certainly the Confederate rank and file believed so. They had been fighting the Army of the Potomac, off and on, for two years now and except for the stand-off fight at Antietam in the early fall of 1862 they had won every engagement. In December they had rebuffed the Yankees at Fredericksburg so handily that half of the Southern army did not even have to get into action. In May, at Chancellorsville, they had inflicted an ignominious defeat on foes who outnumbered them at least two to one. Now, invading the enemy heartland, they had won the first engagement decisively, inflicting ruinous losses and driving the Northerners away from their defensive positions. There seemed to be every reason to believe that the next twenty-four hours might see the job finished once and for all.

Yet the situation was not as rosy as it looked. Winning the first encounter, Lee had in fact put himself in a position where he would have to fight at a disadvantage. For the first time in this war the Federal army—larger than the Army of Northern Virginia, as was always the case—was able to stand on the defensive on its own soil. Lee would have to force the fighting all the way.

The pressure of time was on him and not on his opponent. Lee

Lee

35

could not stand his ground and wait for the Federals to attack; living off the country as it was, his army had to keep moving, and unless it went back to Virginia immediately, tacitly admitting that the whole invasion had failed, it could not move until it had beaten the Army of the Potomac. It could not wait for the enemy to put himself in a false position and then pounce upon an exposed fragment, and it could not let the enemy wear himself out in a fruitless assault and then strike a crippling counterblow. It had to fight right there and right then—on the enemy's terms.

Furthermore, there was no possibility for the kind of maneuvering at which Lee excelled. Jeb Stuart was still not there, and without him Lee could not put his army on the march; if he did, he had no way to tell what he might run into. General Longstreet, stoutest of his corps commanders, had this impressed upon him as this day began.

Longstreet came up to Lee's headquarters in advance of his corps, which had camped for the night a few miles to the west and would be up fairly soon. Longstreet listened to the accounts of the first day's fighting, took in as much of the general situation as could be seen from the ridge where the Lutheran seminary was, and then proposed that Lee move around to the south, circling past the Union left flank and striking for Meade's rear. Logically, this was the correct move, and it was in fact what Meade feared Lee would do; but Lee could not do it because under the circumstances it would have been wildly rash. He did not know where all of Meade's army was, he had no way to find out, and if he tried a flank march now he might run into a ruinous ambush.

He had at last learned where Stuart was—he had got his cavalry corps up in the neighborhood of Carlisle, miles to the north, where it was not needed at all, and he and his horsemen would be on hand tomorrow; but Lee needed him today, this morning, and he was not going to have him. Without him he could not make the move Longstreet was urging, and he answered Longstreet in the only way he could answer: "No. The enemy is there and I am going to fight him there."

Lee outlined his battle plan without delay. He would strike at Meade's flanks, trying to crush both ends of his line simultaneously.

To be sure, the Federal position was powerful, but Lee's army had the habit of victory, and Lee seems to have been confident that it could sweep everything before it, once it struck with all its might. He told Longstreet to lead his corps down behind Seminary Ridge and prepare to attack to the eastward. At the same time Ewell would assault the high ground that had not been taken the night before; and Hill, in the center of the line, would lend a hand in either of these assaults or move forward on his own, as circumstances might indicate. The fighting was to begin as soon as Longstreet got his men into position.

It took several hours to do this, and after the war many Southerners bitterly criticized Longstreet, saying that he sulked because his own plan had been rejected and complaining that he could have moved much more rapidly if his heart had been in it. Sulky, Longstreet undoubtedly was, but he does seem to have moved as rapidly as possible —after all, it took time to get 12,000 infantry men off the road, move them cross-lots through wooded country, and then shake them out into a battle line ready to make a co-ordinated charge. It might be noted that to the end of his life Lee did not criticize Longstreet's behavior on this day. In any case, Longstreet was ready by midafternoon or thereabouts and the great battle of the second day began.

Meade's army was fully confident. For the first time it was fighting on its own soil, and every soldier realized that the job now was to hold on and let the enemy force the fighting; all in all, the men believed that they were going to win this one, and if they drew no especial inspiration from Meade's leadership that did not matter. From first to last, the generals who led this army owed more to the private soldiers than the soldiers owed to them. The men carried within themselves whatever the mysterious quality is that enables a soldier to surpass himself on the battlefield.

The Federal position was strong. Hancock had been right when he told Meade that this was a good place to fight a battle, and Meade— who had reached the field around midnight on the night of July 1— fully agreed once he had studied the layout.

The Federal right was posted on Culp's Hill, a massive, wooded height southeast of Gettysburg. This was held by the XII Corps under

Major General Henry W. Slocum, and on the corps' left, occupying slightly lower ground that swung westward just south of Gettysburg to the high ground of Cemetery Hill, were elements from the shattered I Corps. (Meade was not satisfied with the way Doubleday handled the corps and appointed Major General John Newton to replace him.) Cemetery Hill and the high ground around it was held by Howard and his XI Corps, with artillery posted to sweep the approaches. South from this strong point went Cemetery Ridge, a more or less open stretch whose height diminished as it ran south, and here the II Corps, under Hancock, was stationed, with General Dan Sickles' III Corps on its left.

Major General George Sykes and the V Corps were in immediate reserve, ready to reinforce any part of the left, and coming up from the rear was the reliable VI Corps led by Major General John Sedgwick. It had been far to the east when the order to bring the army together went out, and it was now making a tremendous forced march under a blistering July sun. It probably would not be ready for much action today, but it would be a powerful reserve in case anything went wrong.

The army's left was supposed to be anchored on rocky heights a couple of miles south of Cemetery Hill—Little Round Top, a craggy knob at the foot of Cemetery Ridge, and Big Round Top half a mile to the south. But General Sickles, who held the left, suspected that the Confederates were about to attack him and believed he would be in a stronger position if he moved forward to elevated ground along the Emmitsburg road, half a mile or more to the west of the ground he had been ordered to occupy. He asked for Meade's permission to move forward, failed to get it, and then moved out on his own hook, posting one of his two divisions on the Emmitsburg road facing west and the other one in a peach orchard and a wheat field facing almost south. He had no sooner got them established there than Longstreet opened his attack.

Longstreet was deliberate in getting into position, but when he did strike he hit with great power. He was fighting with only two of his divisions today, under Major Generals Lafayette McLaws and John B.

Lee's major effort in the battle of July 2 was a furious attack by Lieutenant General James Longstreet's I Corps on the Union left, which Major General Dan Sickles, commander of the III Corps, had advanced to the Emmitsburg road, the peach orchard, and a wheat field—a salient jutting out a mile in advance of the position on Little Round Top and lower Cemetery Ridge which Sickles had been ordered to hold. Longstreet's men struck this salient with tremendous power, breaking the defending force and threatening to destroy the entire Union position. This unfinished sketch by an artist catches one of the desperate moments when a Union battery, in the center of the picture, supported by infantry, tries desperately to hold the ground in the face of a Confederate attack coming from the right and right-center of the picture.

The Devil's den
Gettysburg.

Vincents brigade driven in

Some of the worst fighting of the battle came on the afternoon of July 2
when Longstreet's men drove Federal defenders out of a tangle of rocky
ground known as the Devil's Den. Here a battlefield sketch of the beginning
of this Federal defeat catches the sense of confusion that possessed this disordered part of a desperate field.

Hood; his third, Pickett's, had been doing rear-guard duty around Chambersburg, and although it was on its way to Gettysburg, it would not be ready for action until tomorrow—when, as a matter of fact, there would be more than enough grim work for it to do. Longstreet was putting between 12,000 and 14,000 men into action and he struck Dan Sickles' corps with overwhelming force.

The defects of Sickles' chosen position were revealed at once, and many good Union soldiers paid with their lives for this general's lack of battlefield savvy. From the southwest Longstreet's artillery pounded the angle of Sickles' line, and while Hood's division swarmed in against the southern face of the line, McLaws' division attacked the western face. In effect, Sickles was struck on three sides at once, and his undersized army corps was swamped. Sickles himself was carried off the field with one leg shattered by a cannon ball, and Confederate General Hood was disabled by a painful wound in the arm; but the fury of the Confederate attack and the tenacity of the Federal resistance were not diminished, and the battle rose to an unendurable intensity.

Meade ordered one of Hancock's divisions to come to the rescue; then, when the Federals were driven out of wheat field and peach orchard and tried stubbornly to hold on in a formless jumble of rocks and scrub trees south of the wheat field—the soldiers called this place "the Devil's Den," and they named it well—Meade told General Sykes to bring the V Corps into action.

Sykes's men were veterans, and in their ranks was a division of regulars, who gave a special flavor of disciplined toughness to the entire corps. The regulars were shock troops fit for any emergency, but the whole left of Meade's battle line had come unraveled and to stitch it together again under fire was almost impossible. The first essential was to find a secure anchorage for the left flank, and the only possible spot for this was Little Round Top, the hill which Sickles had so blithely abandoned when he moved forward to what he thought was a better position. Hood's troops now were in the Devil's Den, moving on for Little Round Top. If they took it, Meade's entire position on Cemetery Ridge would be untenable and the battle would end in a smashing Confederate victory.

In the Devil's Den and on Little Round Top the soldiers protected themselves as well as they could by piling rocks into crude breastworks. The photograph above, taken immediately after the battle, shows a lifeless Confederate sharpshooter in one of the niches in Devil's Den; the other two photos show Union defenses on Little Round Top.

Apparently there was nothing to keep them from doing it, because the only Federals on Little Round Top just then were members of a Signal Corps detachment. Luckily, however, Meade had sent one of his ablest staff officers, Major General G. K. Warren of the Engineers, down to the left to see what was needed and Warren went to the top of the rocky little hill to survey the situation. What he saw was an advancing line of Confederates, coming out of the trees and shrubs at the edge of Devil's Den and splashing across a little creek that flowed past the foot of Little Round Top, and they carried final defeat for the Union cause on their bayonets. Warren galloped off pell-mell for reinforcements.

By good luck he ran into one of Sykes's advancing brigades whose commander recognized him and knew that any orders Warren might give him would come with Meade's authority, and when Warren told him to get his men to the top of the hill he obeyed promptly. Next Warren found a battery of field artillery, and by dint of enormous exertion—the slope was steep and rocky, and there was no road—the men got these guns up to the crest . . . and by the narrowest margin imaginable the Confederate attack was beaten off. Then additional Union troops were sent farther south to take possession of Big Round Top, and in the end Meade had a solid anchorage for his left. But as the Duke of Wellington remarked after the battle of Waterloo, it had been a damned near thing.

The crisis was by no means over. The Round Tops were at last secure, but the whole area between them and Hancock's position on the upper end of Cemetery Ridge was a no man's land. Longstreet's attack had not yet lost its impetus, a division from Hill's corps was coming into action from the west, on Longstreet's left, and bits and pieces of three Federal army corps were eddying about under heavy fire trying to find a rallying point. At one place nothing but an improvised line of Federal cannon, devoid of any infantry help whatever, held the ground; at another a Confederate charge was beaten back when Hancock called on one of the army's best regiments, the 1st Minnesota, to make a counterattack all unsupported. This prevented a Confederate penetration that might have wrecked everything, but the 1st Minne-

44

sota was all but destroyed, losing more than 80 per cent of its men. A little farther north, some of Hill's soldiers seized a rank of guns on the very crest of Cemetery Ridge, but Meade was getting reinforcements to the scene and these Southerners at last had to retreat. When darkness at last descended, the Union left was holding its ground and apparently could continue to do so, but the men had never had to fight any harder than they fought this afternoon.

At the other end of the line, the extreme Union right, the fighting had been equally severe. Ewell's men had gone valiantly up the steep wooded slopes of Culp's Hill; not only had the ground not permitted effective use of the dominant Federal artillery, but Meade had also had to take troops from this hill to buttress the line on Cemetery Ridge, and his defense here was under strength. The Federals were well dug in, however, and they were good men—they belonged to General Slocum's XII Corps—and they beat off four consecutive attacks without giving ground. But if the Confederates could not quite get to the crest of the hill, they were of no mind to give up, and when darkness came they held a ragged line halfway up the hill, overlapping the Union right and in excellent position to drive past it into the Union rear. It was as certain as anything could be that they would renew their offensive as soon as morning came.

Even the fighting on Culp's Hill did not complete the story. Between Culp's Hill and Cemetery Hill, facing north toward the town of Gettysburg, there was a saddle of higher ground held by assorted Federals, and as dusk came on, the Confederate General Early took his division up a ravine and sent battle lines swinging up the slope against this part of the Union line. There was desperate fighting here, the half-light of evening all clogged with blinding layers of powder smoke, and although the defenders near Culp's Hill beat their assailants off, several Louisiana regiments farther west broke through entirely and overran the XI Corps artillery on Cemetery Hill, driving one of the XI Corps infantry brigades away and threatening to break Meade's line right in half. But the Confederates who attacked here were up against the cruel handicap that operated against Lee's men throughout the last two days at Gettysburg: whenever they got into a Union position

(text continued on page 61)

45

These two contrasting sketches supposedly depict the same part of the battle on the second day—the union repulse of the Confederate drive to take Little Round Top and destroy Meade's left. One picture is of the traditional "picture-book" school, grotesquely unreal, showing orderly ranks of Union troops advancing behind a general who rides valiantly in front waving a flag. The other picture comes much closer to realism, showing the Confederates advancing up the littered hillside by twos and threes and squads, taking cover behind rocks and trees, fighting in a smoky fog in which no parade-ground battle lines were ever visible.

The two hills known as Little Round Top and Big Round Top were not actually very high or imposing, but they dominated the nearby terrain just enough to compel any army that wanted to possess Cemetery Ridge to take them first. This scene, taken shortly after the battle, shows Little Round Top on the left, with the larger hill on the right.

This view of Little Round Top and the views on the next two pages show the craggy rocks and the scrubby trees that marked this part of the field.

One of the axioms of military science in the 1860s was that artillery alone could not hold a position; it had to have infantry in support. There was a time on the Union left, late on July 2, when this axiom had to be disregarded. Sickles' line had been pulverized, and although the Round Tops were being held, the Confederates threatened to sweep in north of them and swamp the disorganized defenders of the southern end of Cemetery Ridge. A hastily assembled line of cannon staved off the assault until infantry reinforcements could reach the scene. Here the artist sketches Captain John Bigelow's 9th Massachusetts battery dashing forward into action.

The furious nature of the fighting on the Union left late on July 2 is indicated by this sketch showing Union artillerists withdrawing a piece by hand. All the horses have been killed, and if the piece is to be saved the gunners themselves have to do the work. This method of withdrawal had one thin advantage. It was easy to stop and fire a round at the oncoming foe, because there was no team to be unhitched and no caisson to detach.

The distinguished sketch artist Edwin Forbes made this drawing of the goings-on atop Culp's Hill on the afternoon of July 2, 1863. No sketch artist could quite catch all of it, and this one is slightly formal, stiff, and unreal; yet the ominous battle smoke does ride above the log breastworks, and if the arriving reinforcements have a picture-book air, there is at least the feeling that they are about to step into something violent and dreadful . . . which is the key to the happenings on that hilltop on that sultry July afternoon.

54

In the fight to save Cemetery Ridge on July 2, Meade's chief of artillery sent in batteries wherever he could find them. Here Lieutenant John Butler's Battery G, 2nd U. S. Artillery, from the VI Corps, in reserve, is driven forward to take part in the fight.

Lee's army attacked savagely on the afternoon of July 2, Ewell striking Meade's right on Culp's Hill while Longstreet assailed his left in front of the Round Tops. Sickles, commanding Meade's III Corps, had unwisely advanced to hold a salient along the Emmitsburg road; his corps was routed and only the timely arrival of Sykes's V Corps, along with reinforcements from other parts of Meade's line, kept the entire left flank from being crushed. In the end, Culp's Hill and the Round Tops were held, a thrust at Cemetery Ridge by part of Hill's corps was beaten back, and an attack by Early, of Ewell's corps, on the ground between Culp's Hill and Cemetery Ridge was repulsed.

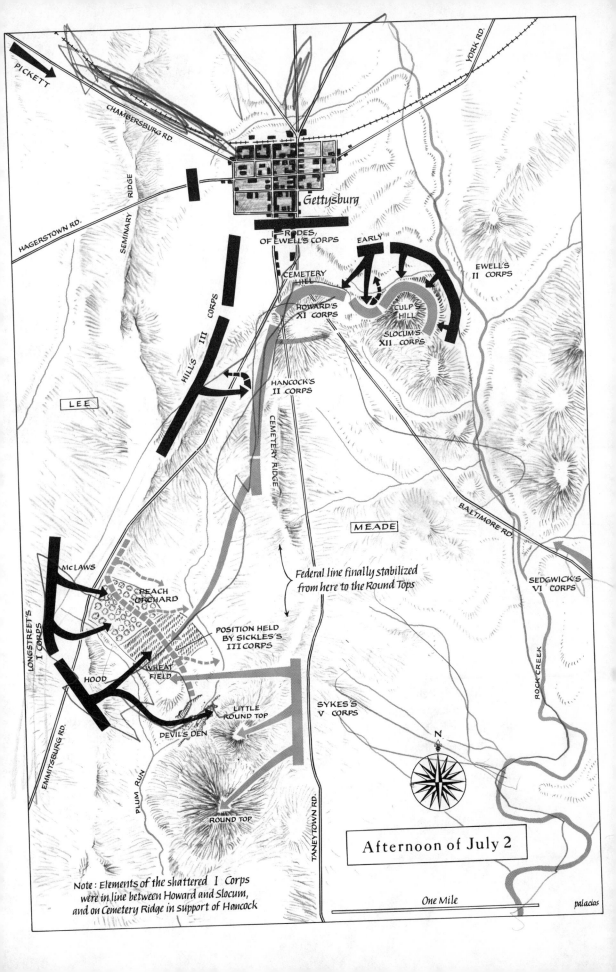

PICKETT

CHAMBERSBURG RD.

HAGERSTOWN RD.

SEMINARY RIDGE

Gettysburg

RODES,
OF EWELL'S CORPS

EARLY

EWELL'S
II CORPS

CEMETERY
HILL

HOWARD'S
XI CORPS

SCULP'S
HILL

HILLS III CORPS

SLOCUM'S
XII CORPS

LEE

HANCOCK'S
II CORPS

CEMETERY RIDGE

BALTIMORE RD.

MEADE

*Federal line finally stabilized
from here to the Round Tops*

SEDGWICK'S
VI CORPS

McLAWS

PEACH
ORCHARD

POSITION HELD
BY SICKLES'S
III CORPS

Longstreet's I Corps

HOOD

WHEAT
FIELD

LITTLE
ROUND TOP

SYKES'S
V CORPS

ROCK CREEK

DEVIL'S DEN

EMMITSBURG RD.

PLUM RUN

ROUND TOP

TANEYTOWN RD.

N

Afternoon of July 2

Note: Elements of the shattered I Corps
were in line between Howard and Slocum,
and on Cemetery Ridge in support of Hancock

One Mile

palacios

The final Confederate offensive thrust of July 2 came at dusk in the form of a sharp assault on the XI Corps position on East Cemetery Hill and on the slightly lower ground running east from that spot to Culp's Hill. These two sketches, which are hardly more than the artist's shorthand but which do preserve something of the tension of violent action, show the Federal battery position and the charge of the Louisiana brigade which came close to seizing and holding this position.

The picture shows the rocky slopes and gloomy woods along the base of Little Round Top. Confederate troops from Longstreet's I Corps made a desperate assault which, if successful, would have destroyed Meade's battle line and given General Robert E. Lee a sweeping victory. Here is a glimpse of the desolate battleground, photographed just after the battle had ended and before the dead bodies had been buried.

they moved farther and farther away from their own army and closer and closer to the Union's reserve forces, so that it was impossible to exploit their success. Now, as full darkness was coming in, and the fighting lines could be marked only by the pin-point sparkles of flame from infantry muskets, Hancock sent a brigade over to the rescue and it struck the Louisianians with paralyzing force, drove them back to their own lines, and restored the situation for Meade.

Late that night, with a full moon shining down grotesquely through the smoke-stained air and the night all clamorous with the cries of wounded men calling for help—the July heat was a heavy burden, and the wounded men desperately wanted water—Meade held a council of war in the little farmhouse on the eastern slope of Cemetery Ridge that served as his headquarters. One after another his corps commanders made their reports: they had had a tremendous fight and losses had been frightful, but they believed they could hold their ground if Lee renewed the attack tomorrow. (To a man, they expected him to do so. They had seen enough of him by this time to know that he could be counted on to go on fighting as long as a chance of victory remained.)

Meade did not need to reflect very long. He had had his chief of staff prepare tentative plans for withdrawal, in case worse came to worst, but he had no intention of using them unless he had to, and although he had lost 20,000 men thus far he sensed that this fight was costing his opponent even more and he knew that his own cue was to stay where he was. He made up his mind to do the obvious thing—hold on, and if Lee did not attack, go over to the offensive—and he told one of Hancock's generals that he expected Lee to attack the Union center on July 3. When the general asked why he looked for this, Meade remarked that Lee had struck both flanks and failed: the center was the only objective left.

As it happened, the center—the ground along the upper part of Cemetery Ridge, where the ridge joins Cemetery Hill—was the strongest part of the Union line, and that Meade should expect Lee to strike him there showed that he had an intuitive understanding of the compulsion under which the great Confederate general was laboring at Gettysburg.

61

Veterans of the Civil War said that a battlefield could show no more hideous sight than the mangled corpses in front of a place that had been defended by close-range artillery fire, which tore human bodies as musketry could not do. Here is grim testimony to the truth of this statement. The photograph was made, apparently, on the Union left.

62

Late at night on July 2, after the dreadful fighting of the second day had come to an end, General Meade held a council of war in his farmhouse headquarters on the reverse slope of Cemetery Ridge. Here he found that his generals felt just as he did—that the army should hold its ground and repel the final assault that Lee would inevitably make next day. Orders were issued accordingly. Afterward, some of Meade's political enemies spread the story that he had prepared to retreat and actually drew up orders for a withdrawal, but this was eventually exposed as a false tale; among others, adherents of General Sickles, who was being criticized for his unwise advance in front of the Round Tops just before Longstreet's assault struck him, tried to restore their general's reputation by undermining Meade's.

The Union position on East Cemetery Hill was retained, finally, when a brigade from Hancock's II Corps came over and drove the Confederates out of the ground they had seized among the guns. The artist who prepared this picture back in New York believed that the scene looked like this.

By sunset of July 2 the Federal position on the left was fairly well stabilized; much ground and many lives had been lost, but Longstreet's powerful attack had at least been contained, and reinforcements had been sent forward to replace the men who had fallen or who had been driven away. Here is a graphic sketch of the position as seen from Little Round Top as the afternoon was drawing to a close.

On the day after the battle ended, an artist made this sketch of relaxed Union soldiers behind their log-and-rock breastworks on the slopes and at the base of Culp's Hill, the anchor for the Union right.

Lee could not withdraw from this battle without admitting outright defeat, he could not simply hold his ground and wait for the Federals to come over to the offensive, and the armies were locked together too tightly to permit the kind of maneuver that Longstreet had called for. Lee was compelled to strike one more blow on July 3, and he had just strength enough for one more blow: Pickett's division had at last come up and could be used for the final stroke of Lee's offensive battle. Ewell's men, who had assaulted Culp's Hill so valiantly, had by no means fought themselves out. If Pickett, suitably reinforced by units from other commands, struck a hard blow at the center while Ewell renewed the assault on Culp's Hill, the day might well be won.

So it looked on the night of July 2, while soldiers from both armies wandered about the field looking for wounded comrades, and uneasy skirmishers kept up a spat-spat of rifle fire on the low ground beyond Culp's Hill. And what nobody quite noticed at the time was that Robert E. Lee was fighting this battle in a manner unlike any he had followed before. His army had become a superb instrument for finding and exploiting enemy weak spots, and over and over again it had won battles against superior numbers by behaving in that way. Now, for the first time, it was hitting the enemy's strong points; in effect, it was fighting Meade's way, not Lee's. Coming north of the Potomac, the Army of Northern Virginia had mislaid its old recipe for victory.

IV
Third Day: Climax

In a way the story of Gettysburg is the story of the country roads that come to the place. They were unpaved roads in 1863, white and dusty under the July sun, binding town to countryside, knitting the Pennsylvania townships together, unremarkable and unknown to fame; bearing now a strange traffic. Thousands of men tramped along them to meet what was waiting at the end of the last hard mile, stepping off the map altogether, stumbling painfully onward and winning a soldier's apotheosis on hills and fields that sandwiched three days of violence in between unbroken generations of peace to make the more perfect union the nation's elders had dreamed of.

The nation gained unity and an immortal legend because the soldiers followed these roads. What the soldiers themselves gained is not quite so clear, but now and then the haze of the dead years thins out and shows us a few of these young men and we are left with long thoughts. One young man we can get a look at was named Wesley Culp. He was born in Gettysburg, in a house on Culp's Hill—his family gave its name to the place and had its home under the trees on top of it—and in his early teens Wesley Culp left home and went out into the world to seek his fortune. He settled somewhere in the upper Shenandoah Valley, and when the war came he considered himself a Virginian and enlisted in the Confederate army. He came back to Gettysburg as an infantryman in General Ewell's II Corps, and when the men of that corps tried to win the battle by capturing Culp's Hill he was in one of the assault waves. He was killed within a few yards of the house where he was born, and at your leisure you can try to appraise the ins and outs of his tragic fate.

Another soldier who comes in for a brief close-up is young Colonel Strong Vincent, who commanded a brigade of Union infantry in General Sykes's V Corps. On the night of July 1 he was leading his brigade north toward Gettysburg on a driving forced march, and the men were on the road long after night came. There was a bright moon, and when the brigade came to a little town, the regiments broke out their battle flags and set their bands playing, and in every doorway and shadowed yard there were girls waving and cheering. Colonel Vincent reined in his horse while the column went through the town, doffing his hat as the flags passed him, looking at the town and the girls and the soldiers, and to an aide he remarked that there could be a worse fate than to die fighting here in Pennsylvania with the flag overhead. . . .

Then he resumed the march along the road to Gettysburg: the long road white in the moonlight, with the small-town girls laughing and crying in the shadows and the young men waving and passing on. To the girls who had been nowhere and had all of life ahead of them, this was the first of all the roads on earth, and to many of the young men it was the last road of all—and to girls and boys alike, equally, it led to unutterable mystery. It was the last road for Strong Vincent, because the next afternoon, when General Warren rode desperately to find troops to hold Little Round Top, Colonel Vincent's brigade was one that was sent there, and Vincent lost his life in the way he had chosen, fighting on Pennsylvania soil under the national flag . . . defending a rocky hillock that had to be held if the union of the states was to survive.

Lee had come over the Chambersburg road from the west, riding up the long slope of South Mountain and then coming down to the clamorous plain with its great streaked blanket of battle smoke hiding the future and all its chances. Meade had come up the Emmitsburg road from the south to see the battle his advance guard had prepared for him, and they may have told him how the first Federal infantry, the Iron Brigade (wrecked now almost beyond repair), had left the road just below Gettysburg to go cross-lots over to Seminary Ridge, where

Yankee cavalry was trying to hold off Confederate infantry. The Federal commander had sent the fife and drum corps to the head of the column to play the men into their last great fight, and it played "The Campbells Are Coming," the fifes shrilling out above the hard clatter of musket fire, the rattle of drums jarred off balance by the heavy concussion of artillery fire. . . . There had been hard fighting that day of July 1, and harder fighting on July 2, and now it was July 3 and time for this bloody business to come to its climax.

The climax was approaching fast enough, but it was not coming quite as Lee had planned. He would send Pickett and his division against the Union center, with good fighting brigades from Hill's and Longstreet's corps to help out, making a charging column of somewhere between 10,000 and 15,000 men; and when they struck the center, Ewell would renew his assault on Culp's Hill, and Stuart's cavalry—on hand at last, days late—would curl far around the Union right and disrupt the Union rear. It was a good plan, and it might well succeed; from Lee down to the last private, the Army of Northern Virginia believed it was irresistible' when it hit with all its strength. But co-ordination was lacking, this third day of July, and the timing was off.

It took time to get Pickett and the supporting troops in position, and Ewell's men could not wait. They had made an uneasy bivouac halfway up the slopes of Culp's Hill, and when dawn came they inevitably renewed their fight without waiting for further orders. General Slocum, the Union commander whose lines included Culp's Hill, had had to send half of his corps away the evening before to help buttress the Union left, but he had got his men back during the night and reinforcements were at hand, and when the fighting flared up this morning he was ready for it. It was savage while it lasted, but the Union position was strong and Slocum's soldiers blistered the aisles between the trees with deadly musket fire, and long before the morning was over the Confederate assailants had to give up and retreat to the plain below. The attack on the hill was over, once and for all, before Pickett's men were ready to begin.

So there was a strange hour of tense, uneasy quiet at noon on

July 3. Destiny was taking its time. As the morning wore away the great battlefield became almost hushed. Off to the east the last sound of the assault on Culp's Hill died away. Down by the Round Tops, Devil's Den, and the peach orchard firing had ceased. There was a brief flare-up, once, west of the place where the national cemetery now lies, when Federal and Confederate skirmishers and gunners contested briefly for a barn between the lines which made a good hiding place for sharpshooters. This fight swelled to a brief fortissimo, the barn took fire and was burned, and then the unimportant struggle ended. A haunted quiet developed, with a sense that a fuse was inexorably burning toward a mine.

George Gordon Meade knew no better than anyone else what was going to happen. He was certain only that he was ready for it, whenever and wherever it might come, and that his army was equally ready.

The weather was almost unbearably hot today and Meade was weary. To him, at noon, came an invitation to lunch. Brigadier General John Gibbon, commanding a division in Hancock's corps, had a meal ready on the reverse slope of Cemetery Ridge no great distance from Meade's headquarters. Meade rode over and, with Gibbon and Hancock and several staff officers, lounged on the grass to eat boiled chicken and potatoes. (The chickens, as Gibbon remembered, were good enough but somewhat tough.) After lunch Meade went back to his headquarters. Hancock called a clerk and began to dictate an order regarding commissary arrangements. A little to the west, beyond the crest of the ridge, Union infantrymen sweltered helplessly. Some of them tried to rig shelter-tent halves so as to get a little shade.

And then, suddenly, the great tension snapped.

Down by the peach orchard one of the Confederate field guns was fired, the sharp clang of the discharge echoing across the still field, while a puffball of white smoke drifted lazily up toward the sky, and Federal artillerymen on Cemetery Ridge blinked and wondered what the Johnnies were up to now. There was a brief pause, then another gun in the same battery was fired . . . the signal Lee's army was waiting for. All along the Confederate line, out in the shallow open valley west of Cemetery Ridge, from the peach orchard to the rising ground directly west of Gettysburg, there were 140 Confederate cannon, and on the signal the gunners who had been lounging nearby jumped up and ran to their posts. There was a long ripple of movement; then every gun in the Confederate line went off, in one long rolling crash—the loudest noise, probably, that had ever been heard on the North American continent up to that moment. The most stupendous bombardment of the Civil War had begun.

General Hancock and General Gibbon and the staff officers ran to their posts, and a hurricane of solid shot and exploding shell swept across Cemetery Ridge. Meade had read Lee's intention accurately; there was going to be a smashing attack on the Federal center, and this bombardment was meant to cut the infantry line and to break up the supporting artillery, paving the way for the Confederate advance.

General Gibbon wrote after the battle that he and an aide went forward to his division's picket line, down the slope a hundred yards or so west of the crest of the ridge, to see what could be seen of Lee's army. Gibbon found that he could see practically nothing. The whole shallow valley, two miles from north to south and half a mile or more in width, was brim full of boiling, eddying smoke—black smoke rising from the ground like a sluggish cloud, white smoke above it, the whole shot through incessantly by stabbing flashes of flame from guns that could not be seen. The uproar was so heavy and continuous that Union gunners on Cemetery Ridge, opening fire in reply, could not hear the reports of their own guns.

Massive though it was, this bombardment did not quite do what Lee had hoped it would do. The Confederate gunners were firing just a little too high. The waiting Federal infantry suffered comparatively little. ("Comparatively" is the word to emphasize: the sound and fury were wholly terrifying, and when shell exploded among the rocky ledges they sent deadly fragments of stone whirring into the ranks of defenders who hugged the ground desperately.) The Federal artillery got it worse, but the heaviest metal of all fell on the far side of Cemetery Ridge, where wagon and ambulance trains were parked, non-combat details were in waiting, stragglers of high and low degree had taken refuge, and general officers had their headquarters. The far slope which should have been so safe became briefly the most dangerous spot on the battlefield as shell came skimming over the crest to break among people who could not see the firing line. The stragglers, wagon trains, and military stand-bys in general broke for cover, and Meade found it impossible to carry on headquarters business in a little farm house that was continually being pierced by cannon balls. He moved, before long, to General Slocum's headquarters, farther east. While the bombardment lasted, General Gibbon, walking up and down in advance of the front line, found that he could stand erect without undue risk; actually he was much safer than the commanding general back at the supposedly secure headquarters.

No one really knows how long the great bombardment lasted, and the estimates (made by various men who lived through it) ran all the way from thirty minutes to two hours. It did end at last, as the Confederate stock of ready ammunition began to run low; so the Confederate fire faded, and the answering fire of the Union gunners died down as well, and slowly the great smoke bank lifted from the valley and men could see again.

Along Hancock's defensive line on the ridge Union soldiers looked to the woods that fringed the opposite ridge a mile to the west, and as the guns fell silent they could see a long ripple of movement, and men with rifles and flags stepped out into the open. The Federals saw, knew that the real test lay not far ahead, and muttered to one another:

"Here they are. Here comes the infantry."

Military men then had, and still have, a succinct expression: infantry is the Queen of Battles. Cavalry was very useful, and there were many jobs where powerful artillery was essential, but when the final showdown came the foot soldier carrying a rifle was the important figure. The big guns had done what they could; now it was the infantry that would settle matters.

The open hollow between the ridges was the great valley of the shadow of death, and when the smoke drifted up and spun away into misty fragments it was as if a curtain had gone up to reveal the stage of some terrible unimaginable theater. The Federal soldiers on the eastern ridge looked west; they were veterans and they had been in many battles, but what they saw now took their breath away. Some of them had seventy-five years yet to live and some of them had no more than ten minutes, but until they died they remembered the scene that now presented itself. There it was, for the last time in this war, perhaps for the last time anywhere, the fearful pageantry and color of war in the old style, beautiful and majestic and hideous; fighting men lined up in double and triple ranks, a solid mile from flank to flank, slashed red flags overhead, sunlight glinting off polished musket barrels—the flower of Lee's army coming forward, unhurried, for the great test that would determine whether there would hereafter be one nation or two between Canada and the Rio Grande . . . and whether Americans on American soil could continue to own other men and women, or be owned by them, as cattle and horses are owned.

The flower of Lee's army: 15,000 men, or perhaps a slightly smaller number, coming along with Pickett's division as the spearhead. Out of the trees and the shadows they came, and when they reached the open they paused and dressed their lines with parade-ground formality, as if they proposed to go about this business of crushing the Yankee host with a flourish in high style, pride and courage blending into arrogance and dauntless confidence. The ranked Confederate cannon were all silent as the infantry passed through, and on Cemetery Ridge the Union guns also were silent, and it was as if both armies waited to savor the war's supreme moment of drama.

The advancing Confederates had nearly a mile to go, and the odds were against them. Tough General Longstreet, who had urged Lee to swing off around the Union left to strike for the unprotected rear, did not think this attack could possibly succeed, and when Pickett rode up to him to say that the ranks were all formed and to ask if he should begin the charge, Longstreet was unable to put the order into words and could only bow his head in a choked gesture of command.

These men were going to march uphill to strike the Union line where it was strongest, and they would be a perfect target. Furthermore, if they themselves were the flower of Lee's army, the men they were about to fight were the flower of Meade's army—Hancock's II Corps, mostly, with unbroken elements from the shattered I Corps, and with the powerful VI Corps available for use if reinforcements were needed. After the war Longstreet said that he had warned Lee that "no fifteen thousand men ever arrayed for battle can take that position," and whether he actually said it or just thought afterward that he should have said it, his appraisal stands. The thing just could not be done.

But the way it was tried still commands attention.

The great charge actually began in silence, as if the two armies consciously willed a lull while the long lines were carefully dressed. The Confederate guns could not fire while the infantrymen were passing through their line, and most of the waiting Federal cannon had used their long-range ammunition in the earlier artillery duel and had to wait until the attackers came close; and the troops were not yet within effective musket range. So the long lines came forward, brimming up to the long diagonal of the Emmitsburg road, crossing it, and pausing once more to perfect the dress. Then they moved on again, and if the waiting Federals looked closely they could have seen a Confederate officer who held his sword high over his head, with his black felt hat on the lifted point of it as a guide for his brigade—Brigadier General Lewis Armistead, who was coming over the valley to meet death and an old friend.

One of the most moving things about this tragic Civil War was the fact that so many of the ranking officers on both sides were close personal friends of the officers whom they had to fight. Before the war the regular army had been comparatively small, and everybody knew everybody else, bound together in a closed professional circle whose intimacy went back to the parade ground and classrooms at West Point and continued through service at isolated little army posts all up and down the west and along the coasts. When the nation broke in half and went to war over it, some of these army officers

General Hancock personally directed the spirited defense of the Union
center, and at the climactic moment the scene may have looked something
like this, making due allowances for the artist's trick of making things seem
more orderly than they really were. Hancock, who was desperately wounded
a few moments later, is on his horse in the left center; directly above him, his
old friend Armistead, hat on sword, may be seen running forward to take possession of a Union gun.

remained in Federal service and others took service with the Confederacy; and the war flung them cruelly against each other, so that a general going into battle might very well find himself confronting his closest friend. And General Armistead illustrated this point perfectly.

Back in the spring of 1861, when the Union seemed to be dissolving and the officers of the old army were choosing their sides, there was a farewell party one evening in the officers' quarters of a little army post outside of what was then the little California town of Los Angeles. The man who gave the party was Captain Winfield Scott Hancock, and the guests of honor were fellow officers who were resigning their commissions in order to enter the army of the Southern Confederacy; among these was another captain, Lewis Armistead, who was one of Hancock's intimates. Late in the evening one of the officers' wives sang "Kathleen Mavourneen," that haunted song of a long parting—"It may be for years and it may be forever"—and then the party broke up and Armistead came over to shake hands with Hancock. Tears were in his eyes, and as he shook Hancock's hand Armistead said: "Goodbye—you never can know what this has cost me." Then he went away, and he and Hancock had not seen each other again. Now Armistead was leading the spearhead of Pickett's charge up Cemetery Ridge, and waiting for him at the crest was his old friend Hancock, with the shotted guns all around him.

When the Confederates formed their lines just before beginning to advance, they had designated a "little clump of trees" on Cemetery Ridge as their objective. It was a wholly unremarkable little grove, hardly big enough for a family to have a picnic in, and it had open fields all around it, with a low fence of stones and rails running along the western side. It lay on the skyline as a good landmark, right in the center of Hancock's line. Here was the spot Pickett's men were to hit, and as the long lines swung across the Emmitsburg road the flanking elements began to move in toward the center so that the entire mass could strike the selected place with maximum impact.

But at about the time the Southerners crossed the road they began to have trouble. Much of Hancock's artillery might be out of action,

The most famous and unremarkable grove in North America is probably the "little clump of trees" on Cemetery Ridge at Gettysburg. This grove stood at about the center of Meade's line, and when Lee ordered an assault on the Union center on July 3 his troops were told to march toward the clump of trees, which made a first-rate landmark. Here is the grove as it looks today.

81

waiting for close range, but when the attackers crossed the road they came within reach of the infantry's muskets, and these were the deadliest weapons of all. The field guns were frightening and under certain circumstances they could be devastating, but in the long run, battles were decided by musket fire and so it was here. As Pickett's men advanced, the right wing of the charging column had to cross an open space beyond which there was a brigade of Vermont infantry, and this infantry moved forward a hundred yards or so, swung to its right, caught the end of the Confederate line in flank and opened a killing fire that shattered the flank and sent the survivors crowding off toward the center. At the same time a long rank of reserve artillery, posted to the south of Hancock's infantry, began to fire obliquely down the length of the Confederate ranks, adding to the carnage. The right end of the assaulting column was crippled before it got to close quarters.

At the northern end of the line there was a similar story. Some Ohio troops had worked their way forward, like the Vermonters farther south, and these caught the Confederate left flank with a shockingly effective fire. Along the low stone wall facing the Confederates on this part of the field were Union soldiers armed with smooth-bore muskets in place of the rifled pieces that were standard equipment; but the range now was so close that the smooth-bores (charged with buckshot, they were today, usually with an overload) could have full effect, and the Confederates were under terrible fire from two sides.

Then the Union artillery got into the action again. There were plenty of guns here, off a few hundred yards to the north of the little clump of trees, and if they had used up their long-range ammunition, they had plenty of canister, and now they got off a furious blast. (Canister was the gunners' close-range ammunition; a charge of canister consisted simply of a tin can full of lead slugs somewhat smaller than golf balls. When the gun was fired, the tin can disintegrated and the slugs went out in an expanding cloud, like a charge fired from a monstrously over-sized sawed-off shotgun. Within

A low stone wall topped by fence rails ran along the front and sides of the clump of trees and offered a good defensive position for Union infantry. In the ground shown in this picture, extremely quiet and peaceful-looking today, thousands of men struggled desperately at the great climax of the battle on July 3, when Major General George Pickett's charge reached this point, hung on there for a moment, and then broke up in defeat.

The climax of the battle came on the afternoon of July 3, when some 15,000 men under general control of George Pickett struck Hancock's position on Cemetery Ridge after 140 Confederate guns had carried on an intensive bombardment. Aiming to strike the center of Hancock's line, with a "little clump of trees" as their landmark, the Confederates struck a position too strong to be carried with the numbers available, and their costly repulse ended the battle. Earlier, Ewell had unsuccessfully attacked Culp's Hill, while Union and Confederate cavalry fought a sharp but essentially meaningless engagement east of Gettysburg.

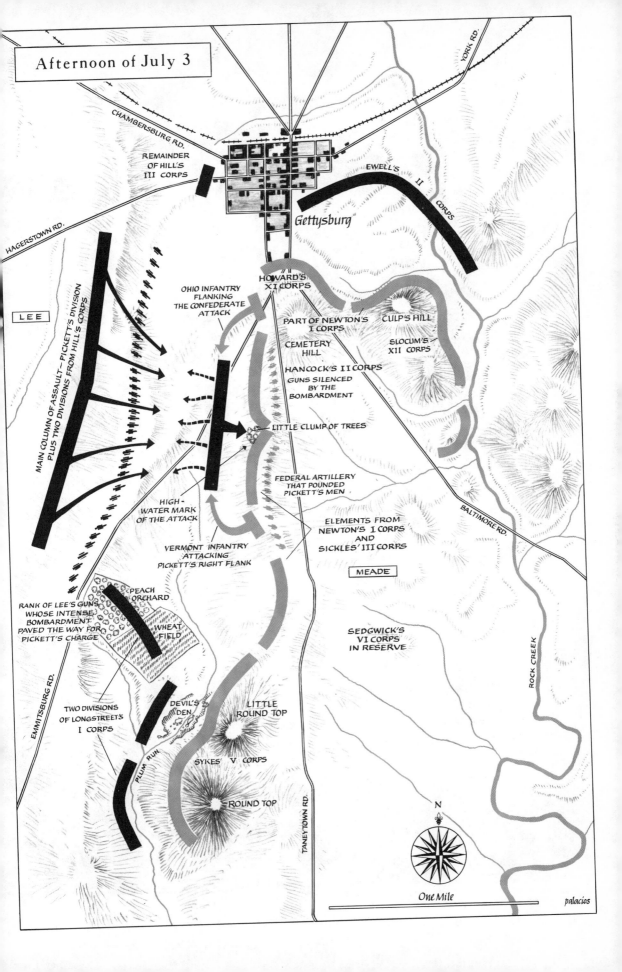

Afternoon of July 3

CHAMBERSBURG RD.

YORK RD.

HAGERSTOWN RD.

REMAINDER OF HILL'S III CORPS

EWELL'S II CORPS

Gettysburg

LEE

OHIO INFANTRY FLANKING THE CONFEDERATE ATTACK

HOWARD'S XI CORPS

PART OF NEWTON'S I CORPS

CULP'S HILL

CEMETERY HILL

SLOCUM'S XII CORPS

HANCOCK'S II CORPS GUNS SILENCED BY THE BOMBARDMENT

LITTLE CLUMP OF TREES

MAIN COLUMN OF ASSAULT—PICKETT'S DIVISION PLUS TWO DIVISIONS FROM HILL'S CORPS

FEDERAL ARTILLERY THAT POUNDED PICKETT'S MEN

HIGH-WATER MARK OF THE ATTACK

ELEMENTS FROM NEWTON'S I CORPS AND SICKLES' III CORPS

BALTIMORE RD.

VERMONT INFANTRY ATTACKING PICKETT'S RIGHT FLANK

MEADE

RANK OF LEE'S GUNS WHOSE INTENSE BOMBARDMENT PAVED THE WAY FOR PICKETT'S CHARGE

PEACH ORCHARD

WHEAT FIELD

SEDGWICK'S VI CORPS IN RESERVE

ROCK CREEK

EMMITSBURG RD.

TWO DIVISIONS OF LONGSTREET'S I CORPS

DEVIL'S DEN

LITTLE ROUND TOP

PLUM RUN

SYKES' V CORPS

ROUND TOP

TANEYTOWN RD.

N

One Mile

palacios

The artists have had a field day with Gettysburg for more than a century, and the most they can do is convey the impression of huge masses of men fighting furiously amid smoke and spurts of flame. Here are two conceptions of the supreme moments of Lee's attempt to break Meade's line on July 3. The degree of "realism" inherent in either picture is something for the individual viewer to determine for himself; the last of the men who might have borne personal, eye-witness testimony on the matter died long ago.

200 yards this weapon was murderous beyond belief.) When these guns were fired, men who saw it all said that the advancing Confederates disappeared in a boiling cloud of dust and smoke, in which knapsacks and muskets and horrible fragments of human bodies were tossed high in the air; one Federal soldier remembered that there came from this part of the field a strange sound that was like an agonized gasp of pain coming from hundreds of throats. No one seems to have remembered hearing any cheers from either side. One soldier recalled only "a vast mournful roar" that seemed to rise from the entire field.

Thus, as the great charge drew near to its objective, both its flanks had been broken. (Flanking fire was especially deadly, because the line that was being flanked could not make any reply to it and was itself utterly vulnerable; fire that came slicing along the length of an infantry line simply could not miss, and no troops could stand it very long.) Longstreet, looking on from the rear, saw what was happening and remarked to a British observer who was standing beside him that the attack was going to fail.

But it had not failed yet, and if the flanks of the Confederate line crumbled, the center was strong. It built up its strength now, in front of the memorable clump of trees. (The trees are still there, protected by an iron fence, all set off with monuments and plaques.) As they came in close—whites-of-the-eyes range, at last—the Confederates halted. Standing, kneeling, or lying at full length, they opened their own rifle fire on the Federals. An infantry attack in the Civil War rarely involved an unbroken run forward followed by hand-to-hand work with the bayonet. The object usually was to try to build up an overpowering rifle fire at close range, gaining superior fire power at the point of contact. Even with their broken flanks, the Confederates were accomplishing this here, and along the low wall that marked the Union front just before and to the immediate right and left of the clump of trees there were more Confederates than Federals in action.

For the next few minutes this irregular rectangle of ground, a hundred yards deep by two or three hundred yards wide, was the

One on-the-spot artist visited the Union center on July 4 and sketched this grim picture of wrecked caissons and dead horses in one of the Federal battery positions.

GETTYSBURG: THE FINAL FURY

bloody cockpit of the whole war, the place where men on foot with
guns in their hands would arrive at a verdict. In this rectangle there
was little work by the artillery. The Confederate guns to the west
could not fire into this place without hitting their own men, and the
Union guns here were out of action. A regular army battery of six
guns commanded by Lieutenant Alonzo Cushing had been posted
just north of the trees; by the time the Confederates came up to
close range, five of the six guns had been put out of action, and when
Cushing got off a final shot from the one gun that remained, he was
killed and most of the gun crew went down with him. The climax
of Pickett's charge was an infantry fight pure and simple.

It was fought out with unremitting fury. Some of Pickett's men
broke in across the stone wall and knelt amid Cushing's idle guns to
fire point-blank at the defending infantry. Some of the defenders
found the fire too hot to bear and withdrew; on a narrow front, and
for the moment, Pickett's men had actually broken the Union line.
If they could widen the break and hold on to the ground gained
until help came, they would have the battle won. . . .

Nowadays a visitor can stand by the clump of trees and see the
whole battlefield, and it is hard to realize that hardly anything was
visible to the men who were doing the fighting. This battle was fought
in a blinding fog—a choking, reeking, impenetrable mist of powder
smoke—smoke from the cannon and from the infantry rifles—lying
close to the ground and drifting up toward the sky until some breeze
might carry it away. Directly to the west of the focal point of the
battle Lee himself watched and could see nothing—just an occasional
glimpse of tossing flags and stabbing flames when the smoke would
thin out temporarily. Longstreet ordered a brigade forward to reinforce Pickett, and the men could not see their objective because of
the smoke clouds; they drifted far off to the right, came up against a
waiting rank of Federal cannon and the spirited Vermonters, and
were torn apart and compelled to retreat without having had the
slightest effect on the course of the battle.

Several miles to the eastward Stuart's cavalry had at last gone into
action, striking for the Union rear so that if the infantry assaults

forced Meade to retreat, the Confederate horsemen could harry the fugitives and turn an orderly withdrawal into disordered rout. But the Federals were not retreating, and Union cavalry met Stuart's men, fought hard with charge and countercharge, and at last drove them away. Nothing could help Pickett's men. They would have to fight this one out on their own, there along the crest of Cemetery Ridge, with the broiling July sun shining down on the monstrous cloud blanket that piled thicker and thicker over the invisible scene of the fight.

For a brief time the Confederates had the advantage, but they could not hold it. Crowding in to lay fire on the Federals in and on both sides of the fated little grove, they had an advantage in numbers, but there were too many Union soldiers in the immediate vicinity, and these were called over on the double. They came in swarms, formal military formation lost as they ran up to get into action at close range. The crowd became so dense that some of these reinforcements, halting to open fire on their enemies, hit their own comrades in front of them—just as some of the distant Confederate cannon, reaching out to hurt the Federals, struck down Confederates in the blind confusion. From the crest of Cemetery Ridge, perhaps a hundred yards behind the point of break-through, the Union regiments that had retreated formed ranks anew, regained their nerve, and opened a sharp counterattack. General Hancock, riding up to see that the front was restored, was shot from his horse with a wound that would keep him out of action until the following spring. General Gibbon also was shot down, severely wounded; but the Federal line stiffened and held without further direction, because in the end this was the private soldier's fight.

On the Confederate side it was Armistead who had led the contingent that broke the Federal line. He was still waving his sword, his black felt hat that had been on the point of the sword had slipped all the way down to the hilt; he laid his hand on one of dead Cushing's guns, urged his men on, a great figure of defiance—and then he fell with a mortal wound. An hour later, when Federal stretcher bearers were combing the littered field, he was still alive—

Probably the most dramatic single moment at Gettysburg came when the Confederate Brigadier General Lewis Armistead, his slouch hat poised on his sword, led the heroic surge of men that broke into the Union line and over-ran one of Hancock's batteries near the clump of trees. Here is an artist's conception of the scene. Armistead got two or three hundred of his men through the line, but he himself was killed and most of those who followed him were shot down or taken prisoner.

enough so that he could stammer out a last message to his old friend Hancock. Then he died, while wounded Hancock was being carried from the field. The paths of these two men, which had parted in California more than two years earlier, had crossed again, for the last time.

Then, suddenly, as the men from the North and the men from the South struggled in the dense battle smoke, the climax was passed. The Confederate wave had reached high-water mark and it began to ebb; watching from his post on the western ridge, Lee could see the human debris of a broken charge drifting back down the long slope. Military formations had been broken, but for the most part the men were going back sullenly, not panicky fugitives but soldiers ready to turn and fight if the Federals attempted a pursuit. The Federals made no attempt. They had beaten back the supreme effort Lee's army could make, but they had just about exhausted themselves doing it. They were content to see their enemies go away.

From his headquarters behind the lines Meade rode forward, saw the littered field, and learned that his soldiers had won a great victory. He took off his hat, apparently preparing to give a great shout, then thought better of it and said, reverently, "Thank God!" A mile away Lee rode forward to rally the men who had made the charge, telling them simply: "It is all my fault."

That night, after dark, Lee issued instructions for the organization of a wagon train to carry some of the thousands of wounded men back to Virginia. To an officer who received the orders, Lee said that he had never seen anything finer than the charge Pickett's men had made. If it had been supported properly, he said, it would have succeeded. Then his emotions broke through, and he cried aloud: "Oh, too bad! Too bad!"

Cameras of the Civil War era were not capable of recording action shots, so no authentic photograph of men in combat in the battle of Gettysburg ever existed. The camera did make its record, however. These two scenes show a few of the many thousands killed at Gettysburg, waiting for the burial squads.

V

Long Remember

With the repulse of Pickett's charge there was only one move Robert E. Lee could make. He had to get his army back to Virginia lest it be destroyed outright, as Abraham Lincoln hoped it might be. The bright possibilities that seemed to be open when general and army came north across the Potomac had vanished. What was left was the simple problem of survival.

Facing this problem, Lee did not panic; indeed, he seemed full of confidence. For the moment his offensive power was gone and he had to get away without delay, but he did not propose to be hurried about it and if the Yankees wanted one more fight here he would give it to them. On the night of July 3, while the shattered brigades that had gone storming up the slope of Cemetery Ridge were getting themselves sorted out, Lee ordered a contraction of his lines. Ewell's men were pulled back from the north and east of Cemetery Hill, and Longstreet's troops were disengaged from the tangled thickets and fields in front of the Round Tops; the wagons containing such wounded men as could be moved were started west, heading for the gaps in South Mountain before swinging south for the river crossings; and on July 4 most of the army stood its ground, warily eyeing the Federals on the high ground to the east. The Confederates more than half expected Meade to attack them and more than half hoped he would try it; they had failed in their own attack, and the failure had left the army half crippled, but the men had not a doubt in the world that they could smash any offensive the Union

General Robert E. Lee, looking as always a little larger than life-size . . . the knight "sans peur et sans reproche." (The Bettmann Archive, Inc.)

soldiers might make. If such an attack were made and beaten back, the whole Gettysburg venture would look a good deal less like the Confederate disaster which in fact it was.

General Meade had no intention of making such an attack. His army had fought and won the most prodigious battle of the war, and if the victory had been purely defensive it had nevertheless been decisive. Meade would not risk diminishing the victory by making what looked to him like an unnecessary attack. Lee had to retreat anyway, his entire invasion scheme in collapse, but if his army had been beaten, it was still as dangerous as a wounded panther. Meade would follow it closely, and if a good chance presented itself he would strike, but he would be very cautious. For the moment he would be happy enough to see the Confederate army leave Northern soil.

Most of Meade's men agreed with him, and the Confederates later asserted that they would have had everything to gain and nothing to lose if Meade had gone over to the offensive immediately after Gettysburg. Indeed, the one man who was seriously displeased by Meade's decision was Abraham Lincoln, President of the United States and, under the Constitution, commander in chief of the nation's armed forces. Lincoln from the beginning had seen what the professional soldiers had mostly failed to see—that when Lee cut his ties with Virginia and marched deep into Northern territory he risked losing his whole army. In the North he could be cut off and compelled to destroy himself in a vain fight to escape. The victory at Gettysburg had been notable, but it was only half of the story as Lincoln saw it. One way or another, Lee's army should be kept from ever going south across the Potomac. To rejoice that he had been driven away from "our soil," as so many Northern patriots were doing, was beside the point, and Lincoln angrily asked his private secretary, John Hay: "Will our generals never get that idea out of their heads? The whole country is our soil." . . . The union was endangered, as Lincoln saw it, not because Lee's army was north of the Potomac but because Lee's army existed at all.

Lee got his army down to the Potomac crossings at last, followed by Meade's army but not actively pursued, and because the river was

Retreating from Gettysburg, Lee sent his wagon train (including the wagons loaded with wounded men) roundabout by Chambersburg, and with the bulk of his army cut cross-country to Hagerstown and over to the Potomac crossing at Williamsport. Meade followed on a long arc that led down through Frederick, cutting west via Middletown to come up against Lee's temporary lines at Williamsport. Lee was delayed here because of high water in the Potomac, but he built an impromptu bridge and on July 13 got his army safely across. Meade had ordered an assault for the next day, but when his troops moved forward the Confederate lines were empty. Lee's army had escaped. The momentous Gettysburg campaign had passed into history.

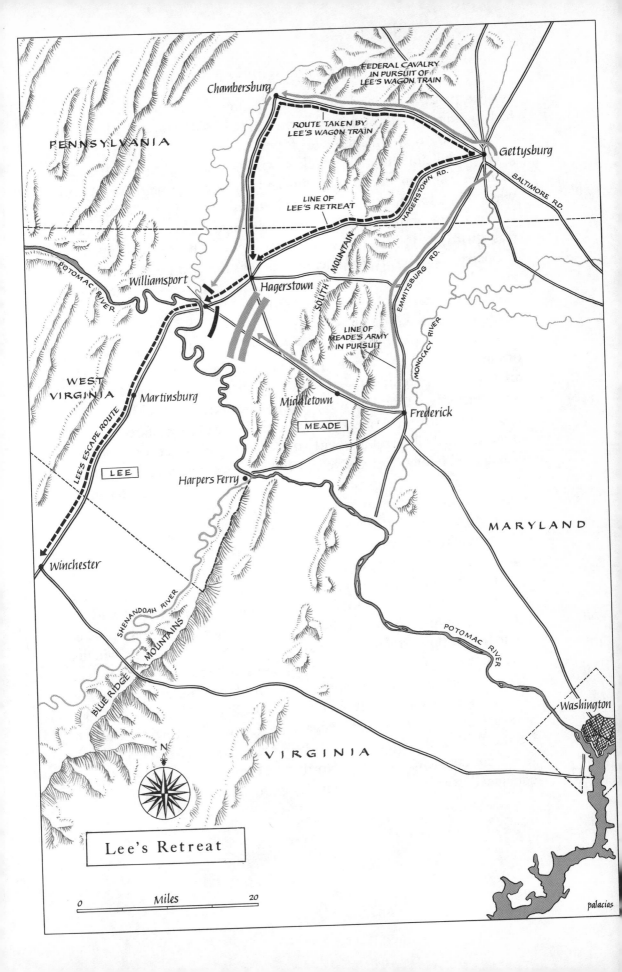

FEDERAL CAVALRY
IN PURSUIT
OF LEE'S WAGON TRAIN

Chambersburg

PENNSYLVANIA

Gettysburg

ROUTE TAKEN BY
LEE'S WAGON TRAIN

BALTIMORE RD.

HAGERSTOWN RD.

LINE OF
LEE'S RETREAT

POTOMAC RIVER

Williamsport

Hagerstown

SOUTH MOUNTAIN

EMMITSBURG RD.

MONOCACY RIVER

LINE OF
MEADE'S ARMY
IN PURSUIT

WEST
VIRGINIA

Martinsburg

Middletown

MEADE

Frederick

LEE'S ESCAPE ROUTE

LEE

Harpers Ferry

MARYLAND

Winchester

SHENANDOAH RIVER

POTOMAC RIVER

BLUE RIDGE MOUNTAINS

Washington

N

VIRGINIA

Lee's Retreat

0   Miles   20

palacios

swollen past fording and Lee had no pontoon train, the Confederates had to wait for a few days, in and around Williamsport. Meade assembled his troops facing Lee, found at a council of war that his generals did not think an attack advisable, made up his mind at last to make such an attack anyway—and on the morning of July 14, when his infantry moved forward to make its fight, learned that Lee had gone across the river during the night, leaving nothing but a rear guard to impede the Yankee advance. The great Gettysburg campaign was over. If, as Lincoln believed, Lee had been in danger of losing his army then and there, he had at last escaped. But in any case this chapter of the war was finished. The invasion of the North had failed, once and for all.

It is easier to see it now than it was at the time, but in fact the great turning point of the war had been reached and passed. Gettysburg drew a good part of its significance from something that happened simultaneously a thousand miles to the southwest. At Vicksburg, Mississippi, on July 4, while the armies in Pennsylvania stared at each other across fields reeking with the dreadful presence of thousands of unburied bodies, General John Pemberton surrendered 30,000 Confederate soldiers, the great stronghold at Vicksburg, and control of the Mississippi Valley to General U. S. Grant. In Lincoln's memorable phrase, the Father of Waters now rolled unvexed to the sea. The Southern Confederacy had been cut in half. Now it could not hope to muster the strength to overthrow the Federal government.

This gave Gettysburg added significance. As Lincoln privately complained, Lee had escaped when he might have been destroyed, but Gettysburg nevertheless had been a prodigious Federal achievement. Here the Confederacy had made its supreme bid to win its independence by a decisive triumph north of the Potomac. It had failed—when all was said and done—had failed because it simply was not strong enough. It could not knock the North out of the war or win the overwhelming advantage that would bring recognition by the British. It might yet win the war, to be sure, by hanging on in a grim defensive until the Northern people and their government concluded that victory was not going to be worth what it would

Lee had just time enough, after the defeat at Gettysburg, to get his army safely south of the Potomac; when Meade assaulted his lines, at Falling Waters near Williamsport, Maryland, on July 13, all but a Confederate rear guard had got back into Virginia. Here the artist depicts an assault on part of the rear guard by a Federal cavalry regiment.

For some thousands of dejected Confederates, the road away from Gettysburg led to a Northern prison camp. Here an artist shows a column of prisoners starting the long march to captivity after the repulse of Pickett's charge on the afternoon of July 3.

cost; but outright victory, forcing the kind of decision the government at Richmond wanted, just was not in the cards. Not after
Gettysburg; not after Gettysburg interpreted in the light of Vicksburg.

For the defeat at Gettysburg exposed a fundamental flaw in Confederate strategy. At least one reason for the invasion of the North
had been the hope that pressure here would compel the government
at Washington to withdraw support from Grant, thereby enabling
the South to save Vicksburg and the Mississippi Valley. This had not
happened. Once Grant got Pemberton and his army locked up in
Vicksburg, Washington sent him strong reinforcements, in men and
in materiel. He lacked for nothing he needed to bring Pemberton to
surrender, and Lee's march into Pennsylvania did not cause
the Lincoln administration to turn a hair. Not one man, gun, or
wagon-load of supplies was withheld from Grant because of the
invasion of Pennsylvania. Even if Lee had actually driven the Army
of the Potomac away from the Gettysburg heights, the Union would
still have taken Vicksburg. This gamble was lost before it was made.

In addition, the Gettysburg campaign had involved the Army of
Northern Virginia in the kind of fight that it had very little chance to
win. Gettysburg had been one of the costliest of battles. In the three
days of fighting the Confederates had lost more than 20,000 men—
slightly less than a third of Lee's combat strength. Federal losses, to
be sure, were higher—at 23,000; but Federal strength was greater,
too, and in proportion to the numbers available the Confederate loss
was heavier than the Union loss.

A year later, when the Army of the Potomac was slowly and
painfully fighting its way south across war-ravaged Virginia, it was
argued that the Union was engaged in a simple war of attrition,
accepting heavy losses for the sake of inflicting heavy losses, knowing
that Northern resources were far greater than Southern resources. As
a matter of fact, the war of attrition had begun much earlier . . . in
the Gettysburg campaign. When the South undertook to invade the
North in the face of Northern superiority in man power, it made a

war of attrition inevitable. Not even Robert E. Lee could win that kind of fight.

The shortcomings of Lee's subordinates at Gettysburg fall into better focus once this fact is appreciated. Ewell might indeed have been dilatory (where his predecessor, Stonewall Jackson, would have moved like jagged lightning) in mounting the attack on Cemetery Hill and Culp's Hill late in the afternoon of the first day; Stuart may have left Lee blind by going far afield and getting his cavalry corps blocked out of the play at the crucial moment of invasion; Longstreet may have been slow, handling his part of the fighting on the second and third days without the furious driving energy Lee wanted—all the complaints on these points, made not by Lee himself but by his admirers, may have been justified. But the hard fact remains that when an army like Lee's took the offensive against a larger army, in the enemy's own country, it committed itself to the wrong kind of fight. At Gettysburg it could do nothing but get in close and slug until something broke. What broke was its own offensive power.

In addition to all other considerations, there is a final point: Lee at Gettysburg was fighting against a man who never wore a uniform or fought a battle: the eminent Illinois civilian Abraham Lincoln. The whole rationale of the Confederate offensive that summer (aside from the purely minor matter of temporarily relieving Virginia of the weight of the war and collecting supplies in Pennsylvania) was the belief that the Northern government would crack under the strain—that it would take troops away from General Grant, lose confidence in final victory when it saw Confederate troops in the Northern heartland, find the price of the war too great to pay, and so consent at last to a formal separation.

None of this happened. The Northern government did not collapse, did not waver in its resolve to go on with the war until slavery and secession were both dead, did not flinch at the fearful price that would still have to be paid . . . and for "the Northern government," read "Abraham Lincoln." He was Lee's ultimate opponent at Gettysburg; he won, partly because Meade and the Army of the Potomac stood firm, but even more because Lincoln himself was where Lee's army could not reach him.

In the fall of 1863, after the armies had gone their ways and entered upon new campaigns, Lincoln himself went to Gettysburg to talk about what had been done there: what had been done, and what it all might possibly mean.

The dead men were all under the ground by now and on the low hill and the long ridge there was the beginning of a great park. There was a formal cemetery, with the soldiers' graves arranged in neat arcs of a series of concentric circles, headstones flush with the ground bearing names and unit identifications . . . hundreds of headstones bearing no names but simply testifying to the presence of bodies that would go forever unidentified. The little clump of trees still stood at the summit of the long slope that came up from the Emmitsburg road, and although it is so small that a couple of good woodsmen could have felled all its trees in one morning, it is nevertheless the most famous little grove in all America. And thousands of Lincoln's fellow countrymen went to Gettysburg for the dedication of the cemetery, and heard famous orator Edward Everett deliver a polished address that left no echoes whatever, and at last stood in silence while Lincoln spoke the few sentences that made cemetery and park something more than a simple memorial to human courage.

No one could explain it better than Abraham Lincoln. When he said that people would never forget what the soldiers had done on this battlefield, he added that no one would long remember what anyone said there; and this was a slight mistake, because what he said there is something the American people will always turn to when they want to know why this great hour of tragedy had to take place and what it meant in the growth of a great nation.

Two or three generations earlier, Lincoln reminded his listeners, the American people had brought forth a nation "conceived in liberty and dedicated to the proposition that all men are created equal." The terrible Civil War itself, he said, was simply a matter of testing whether that nation and the dream that inspired it could go on living. The unlimited potential embodied in the great word "America" depended on the way the challenge was met. The soldiers had done their part . . . to the last full measure of their devotion. The rest, then and thereafter, would be up to the living.

To the living of all subsequent generations, including this one, Gettysburg left an unending responsibility. A nation built on the idea that all men—*all men*—are of equal worth and equal rights summons every one of its citizens to a life-long commitment to put that idea into practical effect.

Gettysburg, then, was the price we paid for our service under that great concept. It was one step in a long progression; not an end, but a beginning—a pledge written in blood that freedom should be reborn in every generation.

So Lincoln explained it, looking across the graves to the truth that gave them meaning. That is why Americans will long remember what was done and what was said on this greatest of their battlefields.

INDEX

INDEX

on July 2, *54, 56, 58*; brief
respite for Union soldiers
at, 66, *66*, 67; Wesley Culp,
birth, soldiery, and death
of at, 71–72; assault on, 73,
74, 84, 108
Cushing, Lieutenant
Alonzo, 90, 91

Davis, President Jefferson, 5
Dedication of Gettysburg
cemetery by President
Lincoln, 109
Defense of Cemetery Hill,
64
Devil's Den, 40; Federal
defeat at, *40*, 41, *42*, 44, 74
Doubleday, Major General
Abner, 24, 25, 28, 38

Early, Major General Jubal,
25, 45, 56
East Cemetery Hill, 58, 64.
See also Cemetery Hill
Emancipation
Proclamation, 6
Emmitsburg road, 38, 39, 56,
72, 78, 80, 109
Engineers, participation of,
44
Evening of July 2, *65*
Everett, Edward, 109
Ewell, Lieutenant General
Richard, 8, 9, 12, 22, 24,
25, 28, 30–31, 37, 45, 56, 67,
71, 73, 84, 99, 108

Falling Waters, Meade
assaults Lee's line at, *105*
Federal Army: I Corps, 18,
20, 22, 24, 26, 28, 78;
II Corps, 64, 78; III Corps,
18, 26, 39, 56; V Corps, 17,
38, 41, 56, 72; VI Corps,
38, 55, 78; XI Corps, 18,
22, 24, 26, 28, 38, 45, 58;
XII Corps, 37, 45;
Massachusetts battery, 9th,
52, *52*; I Minnesota
regiment, 44–45; Ohio
troops, 82; Vermont
infantry, 82, 90
Federal defeat at Devil's
Den, *40*. *See also* Devil's
Den
Federal generals. *See*
Buford; Doubleday;
Gibbon; Grant; Halleck;

Hancock; Hooker;
Howard; Meade;
Newton; Reynolds;
Sedgwick; Sickles;
Slocum; Sykes;
Wadsworth; Warren
Field guns. *See* Artillery,
participation of
Fife and drum corps,
Federal, 73
Forbes, Edwin, sketch artist,
54
Formal cemetery at
Gettysburg, dedicated by
President Lincoln, 109
Forrest, General Nathan
Bedford, 9
Frederick, Maryland:
Hooker's army in vicinity
of, 13; Meade pursues
Lee's army through, 102;
Meade assaults Lee's line
at Falling Waters, *105*
Fredericksburg, battle of, 7–
8, 35

Generals, Confederate. *See*
Archer; Armistead;
Beauregard; Early; Ewell;
Forrest; Heth; Hill;
Hood; Jackson; Lee;
Longstreet; McLaws;
Pemberton; Pickett;
Rodes; Stuart
Generals, Federal. *See*
Buford; Doubleday;
Gibbon; Grant; Halleck;
Hancock; Hooker;
Howard; Meade;
Newton; Reynolds;
Sedgwick; Sickles;
Slocum; Sykes;
Wadsworth; Warren
Gettysburg, Address of
President Lincoln, 109–10
Gettysburg, area around,
endpapers
Gettysburg, battle of:
combination of forces as
causes of, 3, 10, 13, 25;
Lee and, 13, 19; fighting
at, 13, 19, 20, 21, 22, 25,
26–29, 30–31, 72–107;
Buford and, 20; Lee's
men's last two days at, 45–
61; retreat of Lee from,
99, 101–5, 103 (*map*), *105*

Gettysburg, description of
dusty roads and story of,
in 1863, 71
Gettysburg, formal
cemetery at, dedicated by
President Lincoln, 109
Gibbon, Brigadier General
John, 74, 75, 76
Grant, General U. S., 4, 5, 6,
7; surrender of
Pemberton's Confederate
soldiers at Vicksburg to,
104, 107; Washington,
D.C.'s support of, 107, 108

Hagerstown, Lee's retreat
through, 102
Halleck, General Henry W.,
17
Hancock, Major General
Winfield S., 28, 29, *29*, 30,
37, 38, 41, 44, 61, 64, 74,
75, 76, 78, 79, 80, 82, 84, 91,
92, 93; directing Union
defense by, 79
"Hancock the Superb," *29*
Harrisburg, Ewell threatens,
12, 13
Hay, John, 101
Heth, Major General
Harry, 27
Hill, Lieutenant General
A. P., 8, 9, 12, 13, 20, 21,
22, 23, 24, 25, 36, 44, 45, 56,
73
Hood, Major General
John B., 9, 38, 41
Hooker, Major General
Joe, 4, 5, 6, 12, 13; at
Fredericksburg, 7–8; at
Chancellorsville, 8;
replaced by Meade, 10,
17; at Frederick, 13
Horses. *See* Cavalry
participation
Horses, dead, and caissons,
after Pickett's charge, 89,
89
Howard, Major General
Oliver Otis, 18, 22, 24–25,
28, 38

Infantry, participation of, 4–
5, 8, 12, 20, 24, 26, 37, 38,
39, 41, 45, 52, 72, 74, 75,
76, 78, 82, 83, 88, 90